THE COINAGE OF NEPAL

THE COINAGE OF NEPAL

BY

E. H. WALSH

With Scholarly Introductoin

By

Dr. T. P. VERMA

Deptt. of A. I. H. C. & Archaeology
B. H.U.

GYAN

Published by

Gyan Publishing House
5, Ansari Road
Daryaganj, New Delhi-110002
Phone: 011-47034999, 9811692060
E-mail: books@gyanbooks.com

Distribution Network
gyanbooks.com
India, USA, Canada, UK, Australia, France

ISBN : 978-81-212-2858-9 (HB)
First Published, 1973

2nd Impression 2021

Printed at: Gyan Press, Delhi.

The Coinage of Nepal
Author: E. H. Walsh & Dr. T. P. Verma

INTRODUCTION

Not much has been written about the coinage of Nepal since E. H, Walsh published his paper in JRAS in 1908. Recently scholars from both, Nepal as well as abroad, have been attracted towards the subject and some articles have appeared in some journals etc. The coinage as a source of history of Nepal has also been treated by some authors. His Majesty's Government of Nepal has also published 'A Catalogue of the Coins of Nepal' and a book on Nepali coins in Nepali language. S. M. Joshi published his book on Nepal's National Currency in VS. 2017. It seems that the period of collection of coinage of Nepal is over now and a new era of its study and use as a source material for the reconstruction of history has started. One can reasonably hope some scientific studies on the subject in the near future.

The term 'coinage of Nepal' normally means only those coins which were found in the valley of Kathmandu.[1] But in modern times Nepal has comparatively a wide territory under its control. In the year 1768 the Gorkhas conquered the valley and united the three kingdoms to build up a greater Nepal. Within the present frontiers of Nepal there were some independent Kingdoms during ancient and mediaval periods who might have issued their coinage. It is said that towards the hills there are several villages called *takasar*, i.e. mints.[2] If it is any indication one may expect some more coinage, other than those found in the valley which may throw further light on the history of Nepal.[3]

---

1. Walsh ; *The coinage of Nepal J.R.A.S.* p. 672.
2. Joshi, S.M., *Nepālī Rāshtriya Mudrā*, p. 17 fn. 1
3. *Ibid.* p. 46

Stytistically speaking the coinage of Nepal can be classified into two broad divisions. The first group consists of the ancient coinage of the time of the Lichhavis while the second one, started during the Mall rule. Both the groups had separate sources of inspirations and there is a gap of about nine to ten centuries between the two which can be called the 'period of no coins' in Nepal.

As regards the first group all the coins are copper casts. These were inspired by the Gupta coinage of India and were issued under the Licchavi rulers of Nepal. There has been some confusion about the authorship and status of the issuers of these coins. Hence it is necessary to have a look at the political history of the period and to know about the position of the issuers of the coins.

Besides coinage we have two more principal sources of the Licchavi history in Nepal. i.e. the Vamśāvalis and the inscriptions. As the Vamśāvali's are pretty late one cannot solely depend upon their informations which are more confusing rather than helpful in solving any problem. Inscriptions are more reliable and with their help one can have a fairly good idea of the Licchavi history.

The ancient period of the Nepal's history starts with the inscriptions of the Licchavi King Māndeva I whose first inscription, the Chāṅgu Nārāyaṇa Temple Pillar inscription, is dated in Samvat 386.[4] This mode of dating continues upto Samvat 535, in the Jaisideval (Kathmandu) inscription[5] of the time of Sivadeva.

From the viewpoint of dates there is another set of inscriptions the earliest date of this set of inscriptions is the year 30;[6] while the last available date of this set is 207.[7]

---

4. Gnoli, R.: *Nepalese Inscriptions in Gupta characters*, Roma, 1956. No. I

5. *Ibid.* No. XL

6. *Ibid.* No. XXXV.

7. Jha, H. N.: *The Licchavis*, p. 114

There has been much controversy about the identification of the eras used in these inscriptions. As regards the first set of inscriptions the controversy is almost settled now and, the scholars seem to agree to recognise it as the Śaka Samvat starting from A.D. 78.[8] This identification is perfectly in agreement with the historical events so we should not hesitate in accepting it.

The second set of inscriptions is more problematic. Though many of the recent historians are inclined to accept the era to have started in the last quarter of the 6th century A.D., they do not seem to agree about a single date and also about the founder of the era. Dr. D. R. Regmi maintains the initial date as 576 A.D. and regards it as Mānadeva Era. For this he speculates a Mānādeva the Second in 576 A.D. who 'must have a short reign, and a disturbed one. He does not leave us any inscribed steles. Nor his name figures anywhere except in the texts we have quoted.'[10] Śrī J. C. Regmi follows this date. But he accepts the earlier view of Dr. Remi that Aṁśuvarma was the founder of this era[11] He, however, quotes Dr. D. R. Regmi but the latter, as we have pointed out earlier changed his views in the 3rd edition of his book. Dr. H. N. Jha[12] takes the initial date as A.D. 574. One of his arguments is based on 'the Bhīmasena inscription which contains the names of Śivadeva and Aṁśuvarmā is dated Samvat 296. The figure 2 is either misread or misincribed. It should be 4 as all other dates of the inscription of Sivadeva I are found from 517 to 526'.[13] Dr. Jha also regards Aṁśuvarmā as the originator of this era and the usurper of the Licchavi throne.

8. Cf. Majumdar, R. C., *JAS*, Vol. 1. No. 1, 1959, pp. 47-48; Sharma, B, C., *NAR*, p. 82; Regmi, D. R., Ancient Nepal (3rd. Edition) pp. 96-97, Regmi, J. C. *Licchavi Samaskriti* (in Nepali) p. 4 of Introduction; Jha, H. N., *The Licchavis*, pp. 119 ff.

9. Op. cit. p. 109

10. *Ibid*, p. 113

11. *Op. cit.* p. 6 of introduction

12. *Op. cit.* p, 121

13. *Ibid. He refers to Itihasa Prakasha*, pp. 55-56

If the date of the Bhīmasena inscription is 496 (i.e. A.D. 574) it should be regarded as the initial year of the new era as well as the first year of the reign of Śivadeva I. This is in agreement with the Chinese evidence too. A Chinese envoy came to Magadh through Nepal in A.D. 643 and was received cordially by Narendradeva of Nepal whose inscriptions are dated between Samvat 67 and 103. If we accept the initial date of this Samvat in A.D. 574 these dates will fall between A.D. 641 to A.D. 677. Thus the date A.D. 643 of the visit of the Chinese envoy falls during the reign of Narendradeva.

Dr. Jha reached this date through another mode of reasoning also. Sivadeva's inscriptions alongwith Aṁśuvarma are found dated upto the Year 525 (A.D. 604). Aṁśuvarma's first inscription without the mention of Śivadeva, is dated in the Year 30. Assuming this date to correspond with the year 526 of the old era he reached the date of Samvat 496 or A.D. 574 (526-30=496).[14] He argues "it seems that Samvat 526 Aṁśuvarman most probably had completed 30 years of his life as a *Mahāsamanta* to Sivadeva. Again it seems that at the end of the year 526 of the old era or 30th of the new era Aṁśuvarman established a separate kingdom for himself or worked as the regent of Sivadeva, who due to old age or illness, might have been unfit to look after the administration of the country". Dr. Jha further speculates "But the latter suggestion does not show any sense in starting a new era while the old one was also continuing. Hence the greater probability is that Aṁśuvarman established a separate Kingdom for himself and marked its importance by founding an era too. Having not forgotten totally the goodness of King Śivadeva, he did not make any attempt to deprive the latter of having a Kingly life in the old age and continued his title of *Mahāsamanta* at least for some time. After nine years of segregation from Aṁśuvarman, Sivadeva most probably died in 535 (535-526-9 years) and just after his death the former usurped the throne of the latter and dropped his title of

14. *Ibid.* pp. 120 ff.

Mahāsāmanta and issued coins with the title of *Mahārājādhirāja* and Śrī. No coin of his bears the title of Mahāsāmanta."[15]

Tha majority of the historians of ancient Nepal have been the victim of the misconception about the word *Mahārājādhirāja* in the Licchavi records and coins. The title of Mahārājādhirāja for Aṁśuvarmā and coins bearing his name have led the scholars to reason the Aṁśuvarmā was an independent ruler of Nepal. The testimony of Yuan-Chwang that 'Lastly there was a King called Aṁśuvarmā (Ăn-bhu-fa-mo) who was distinguished for his learning and ingenuity.'[16] gave added strength to this conception. But on investigation into the history of ancient Nepal shows that this conception about Aṁśuvarmā is based on wrong notion about the word *Mahārājādhirāja* in the Licchavi inscriptions. It has never been properly interpreted.

Mahārājādhirāja never means a soverign ruler in the Licchavi records. There is only one word in the Licchavi inscriptions which can be said to mean the soverign ruler and that is the *Bhaṭṭārakamahāraja.* This title has always been used for the kings of the Licchavi line only. Liochavis were the *dejure* rulers of Nepal.

But, however, there was an other parallel line of administrators whose constitutional position was perhaps, slightly below the sovereign ruler. They enjoyed full administrative powers depending upon the standing of their individual capacities and ambitions. Perhaps any promotion in their status was dependent on the recognition of the soverign ruler. This second parallel line most probably started in the time of Licchavi ruler Vasantadeva with *Sarvvadaṇḍanayaka mahāpratihāra Ravigupta* and *Mahārāja mahāsāmanta Sri* Kramalīla. The latter contınuded to be in the office during the reign of *bhaṭṭāraka mahārāja* Rāmadeva also. In the line of *bhaṭṭāraka*

15. *Ibid*, p, 121
16. *Ibid*. p. 118

maharāja Śrī Gaṇadeva this poistion was enjoyed by *Varvūadaṇḍanāyaka mahāpratihāra Śrī* Bhaumagupta. He was succeeded by Aṁśuvarmā in the time of Śivadeva.

Aṁśuvarmā started his career under Śivadeva as his *Sāmanta* in or about 574 A.D. This was the inital year of Śivadeva's reign. Then Aṁśuvarmā was promoted as a *mahāsāmanta* and then as *mahārājādhirāja*. The Banepa stone inscription of the time of Śivadeva called Aṁśuvarmā *mahārājādhirāja* and *Sāmanta*.[17] Thus Aṁśuvarmā's title of *mahārājādhirāja* on coins can never mean a sovereign king or ruler or that he usurped the throne for himself. In fact Aṁśuvarmā or his successors Jisṇugupta and Visṇugupta never tried to be independent of the Licchavi rulers. Though, however, it may be surmised that these successors of Aṁśuvarmā were involved in power struggle amongst he main line of the Licchavi rulers. This 'second line of rulers' continued till Licchavi Narendradeva abolished this institution.

Thus there seems no reason to believe that Aṁśuvarmā started a new era of his own.

The continuity of the line of Aṁśuvarmā and his predecessors is indicated in the Licchavi inscriptions. Almost all the inscriptions issued by Aṁśuvarmā, Jisṇugupta and Visṇuguptā begin with the formula *bhagavata paśupati bhaṭṭāraka pādānugrahito-bappa pādānudhyataḥ*. i.e. grateful to the Sovereign *grahīto* god Paśupati and meditating on the feet of father. This latter expression indicates that there was a continuity of succession.

The Kevalpur inscription[18] of the time of Dhruvadeva says that the grandfather of Jisṇugupta was Bhumagupta (Bhaumagupta.) The Pātan (Taujbā Mahalla) inscription of year 48 of the time of Licchavi Dhruvadeva and Jsṇugupta mentions the *bhaṭṭārakamahārājādhirāja Śrī* Aṁśuvarmā in very high spirit. It should be noted that Dhruvadeva succeeded Udayadeva

17. Gnoli, R., *Op. cit.* No. XXXIII

18. *Ibid* ; No. LIV, *asmati; itamahasribhumagutta.*

if we believe in Chinere tradition, and, Jiṣṇugupta succeeded Aṁśuvarmā in their respective positions. Walsh thinks that Jinṣugupta was the son and successor of Aṁśuvarmā.[19] This line continues upto Viṣṇugupta uniterrupted.

But, however, there are certain points in the inscriptions of the period mislead the scholars that this second line rulers was actually independent of their sovereign rulers and some have even suggested the division of eastern portion of the kingdom of the Licchavis and the Western to the line of Aṁśuvarmā.[20] These points are : firstly, issuing of the charters from the *Kaiāsakūṭa Bhawan*, the residence of these secondary rulers : secondly, non-mention of the ruling king's name in his inscriptions by Aṁśuvarmā though his successors do mention their sovereign rulers; thirdly, some of them mention the name of their sons as Yuvarājas (heirapparent), e.g. Jiṣṇugupta and Viṣṇugupta in their charters. These characteristics of the charters issued by the secondary rulere have created much confusion. But a clearer insight into the history of the Licchavis of Nepal, and also on the analogy of traditions of later dynasties of the country, one can have no confusion in understanding the phenomenon.

It is true that Aṁśuvarmā never mentions the ruling king's name in his inscriptions. But his greatest contribution to the Licchavi dynasty is not only in the building up of the kingdom for Śivadeva but also in establishing and using a national era for Nepal which was counted from the first year of the reign of Śivadeva I. Aṁśuvarmā was raised from the position of a *Sāmanta*. a *Mahāsāmanta and Mahārājādhirāja* by the king in recognition of his services to the state.[21] This elevation in position must have been followed by a greater share in administration as. well It is just possible that he was granted the privilege of issuing charters by himself. But he very often mentions *Yuvarāja*

19. *JRAS*, 1908, p. 681
20. Fleet *CII*, Vol. III, pp. 189-90
21. Gnoli, R., *Op. cit.* Nos. XXIII and XXXIII

Udayadeva as *dūtaka* wo was the son of Śivadeva I.[22] Further-more, since Jiṣṇugupta succeeds him as the secondary ruler and one *bhaṭṭāraka mahārāja Śrī* Dhruvadeva was on the throne of the main line there seems on doubt about the continuity of both the institutions and the story that Aṁśuvarmā usurped the throne for himself seems to be a myth.[23]

As regards the issue of the charsters by these secondary rulers from their residence *Kailāśakūṭabhavana*, it seems that the privilege granted as a favour to Aṁśuvarma was continued to be enjoyed by his successors Jiṣṇugupta and and Viṣṇugupta. The mention of their sons and successors as *Yuvarājas* by them also does not seem to be out of place. Since the time of Aṁśuvarmā they were (or got themselves) elevated to the position of *mahārājās* and the tradition of following the convention of the ruling family might have been followed in their family also. There is nothing strange in it. But this does not mean that their *Yuarājas* were the heir apparents to the royal throne. This is evident from the charters themselves that Bhīmārajundeva succeeded Dhruvadeva on the royal throne and in his own turn Viṣṇugupta succeeded his father Jiṣṇugupta in his position. In an inscription[24] of the time of Dhruvadeva while enumerating some past kings Jiṣṇuguṭa inserts the name of his grandfather Śrī Bhamagupta but he clearly mentions that he was his own grand father. This expression of 'our grandfather' (*asmatpitāmaha*) indicates two things. Firstly, that the charters were issued on behalf of the Licchavi rulers, and secondly, that his line maintained a separate succession tradition of its own in their office. As it is evident from the table at the end Bhaumagupta was followed by Aṁśuvarmā, and Jiṣṇugupta in his turn succeeded Aṁśavarmā'. Viṣṇugupta followed Jishṇugupta who was

22. *Classical Age*, p. 136.
23. Cf Jha, H. N., *Op. cit.* p. 121
24. Gnoli, R., *Op. cit.* No. LIV

undoubtedly the latter's son. Mention of Bhaumagupta as the grandfather of Jiṣṇugupta leaves no aoubt that Aṁśuvarmā was his father and predecessor. Thus we can be on comparatively surer footing about their genealogy for four generations. We are at present not sure about Ravigupta and Kramalīlaḥ. Another point wich needs mention here is that every successor of this second line of administrators had to begin with a comparatively smaller position and rose to highest posts after proving his ability. But during the time of Śivadeva I Aṁśuvarmā managed to secure more power for himself and a surer footing his successors. Perhaps after his death Udayadeva, the legitimate successor of the royal throne was caused to leave the country and his younger brother (?) Dhruvadeva was placed there as a puppet king to play in the hands of Jiṣṇugupta. Thus Aṁśuvarmā's successors became so secure in their position that they never bothered to put any title before their name either of a *Samanta* or of *amahārājādhirāja*. Virtuallly they were runāning the kingdom and government. Thus there seems nothing which goes against the view that these were two separate families were continuing in their respective offices for generations the Liccahvavis as the supreme ruling dynasty and the successors of Aṁśuvarmā as their first administrators. Though it seems, they enjoyed more power than the ruling kings but they never tried to usurp the throne for themselves.

A reliable genealogy of the Licchavis can be traced with the help of their inscriptions. The Chāṅgunārāvaṇa Pillar inscription[25] of the Śaka year 386 (A.D.464) of Mānadeva mentions three of his predecessors, i. e. Vṛṣadeva, Śankardeva and Dharmadeva. But the Paśupati Slab inscription cf the year 159 (A.D.833) of Jayadeva II gives an elaborate genealogy starting from Brahmā. 26 This is one of the most misunderstood important inscriptions of Nepal. The first mentioned person who seems of any historical importance

25. *Ibid.* No. 1

26. *Ibid.* No. 1 LXXXI

was perhaps Supuṣpa. But he seems to be a remote name in the geneology of the Licchavis of Nepal. Jayadeva I seems the first person who founded the dynasty but a regular and continuous geneolgy starts from Vṛṣadeva, who was born after eleven kings after Jayadeva I.

Verses 7 to 10 record the names of six kings in succession starting from, Vṛṣrdeva who was followed by Śankaradeva, Dharmadeva, Māndeva Mahīdeva, and Vasantadeva. This statement is in accordance with the description given in the Chāṅgunārāyaṇa pillar inscripiton of Mānadeva for the first three kings. But these first three rulers do not have any inscription to their credit. We find Mānadeva's inscription dated in Śaka years from 389 to 427. The first inscription of Vasantadeva is dated in Śaka 428 and therefore it has been observed that probably Mahīdeva ruled only for few months between Mānadeva and Vasantadeva.

The interpretation of the next verse is most controversial. It gives the names of Udayadeva and his son Narendradeva. The relevant passage runs as follows :—[27]

> *asyantare pyudayadeva iti kshitiśājjātas-trayodaśc itascha Narendradevaḥ.*

Dr. B. L. Indraji translates that "afterwards came thirteen (Rulers) sprung from King Udayadava and then Narendardeva" again, "after him (Vasantadeva) followed thirteen sprung from the Lord of the earth called Udayadeva."[28] But now both the interpretations of Indraji seem unprobable. Fleet seems right in his statement that 'Asyantare can only mean 'in an interval of this.'[29] On this point Dr. D. R. Regmi opines that 'after Vṛshadeva (not after Vasanta) thirteen kings ruled in succession some of whom are named as above and then came Udayadeva being succeeded by his son Narendradeva.'[30] Keeping in view the list of known kings

27. *Ibid.* lines. 10 & 11
28. IA Vol. XIII. pp. 424-25
29. CII, Vol. III, p. 186
30. *Op. cit.* p. 122

given in our table we would like to suggest a slight modification in the view of Dr. Regmi. This should be after Vrshadeva thirteen kings ruled in succession (some of whom are named as above) including Udayadeva and then came (his son) Narendradeve. Thus there ruled fourteen Kings in all including Narendradeva. The record enumerates only eight kings including Udayadeva and his son Narendradeva. The remaining six kings (as supplied by other inscriptions) were, Vāmanadeva, Rāmadeva, Gaṇadeva, Śivadeva, Dhruvadeva and Bhimārjunadeva, Among these fourteen kings all have left records after them except the first three and Mahīdeva (No. 5) and Udayadeva (No. 11). Both of these probably ruled for a very short period. It is also likely that Udayadeva's reign was troubled one. He or his son was some how or the other forced to leave the country and forego his claims. The Chinese sources tell us that the father of Narendradeva was removed from the throne by his younger brother.[31]

For many reasons it seems that the time of Śivadeva I was an important one. R. C. Majumdar[32] observes that 'according to one of the Vaṁśāvalis, the successos of Vasantadeva was defeated by the Ābhīras and after three of their Chiefs had ruled in Nepāl, the Licchavi King Śivadeva expelled them and regained his paternal kingdom. There may be some truth in this tradition?. King Śivadeva can be credited with some sort of great victory after which he installed himself on the Licchavi throne firmaly in Śakayear 496 or A.D. 574 and, this event was credited with the starting of a new era to be used for the first time by Aṁśuvarmā after at least thirty years had passed.[33] Now this has remained a matter of speculation only as to what was the trouble over which Śivadeva gained this memorable victory. It may be the Ābhira trouble or also a trouble from the north. We will

31. Classical Age, p. 136
32. *Ibid*, p. 85
33. Gnoli, R., *Op. cit.* No. XXXV.

again quote Prof. Majumdar who summarises Levi's thoughts as follows:[34]

"Some time between A.D. 580 and 600 the disunited clans of that hilly region had been brought together under powerful ruler, Gnam-ri-sroṅ-btsan, who extended his power upto India. His son and successor Sroṅ-btsan-sgam-po, who introduced Indian civilization into Tibet, is said to have conquered Assam and Nepāl and dominated over half of Jambudvīpa (India). He demanded the hand of a daughter of Aṁśuvarman and the latter dared not refuse."

In the inscriptions of Śivadeva Aṁśuvarmā is repeatedly said to be the destroyer of the enemies.[35] From the very beginning Aṁśuvarmā finds mention in his inscriptions. There is no doubt that it was with the devoted help and assistance of Amśuvarmā king Sivadeva was able to restore peace and stability of his kingdom. Both were long lived; Śivadeva died about A.D. 615 or Śaka 537, and his devoted lieutinent about 619 A.D. or year 45 of the new Śivadeva Era. It seems on account of his modesty Śivadeva did not like to mention the new era but to show his royality and devotion Aṁśuvarmā introduced it in the administration and there was no reason to drop this era by the successors of king Śivadeva. The Licchavi rulers might have returned to the old practice of using Śaka era soon after Narendradeva regained his parental throne. Had the new era been started by Aṁśuvarmā as a result of conflict it must have been rejected and discontinued by Narendradeva who abolished this institution of socalled second line of rulers.

The last inscription of Śivadeva is dated in Śaka 535 (A.D. 613.) In all probability Śivadeva was living in Śaka 537 (A.D. 515 or Year 41 of the new era. His son Udayadeva succeeded him in that year. 'According to the Chinese history the date for Udayadeva corresponds to 615-620 A.D.'[36] In terms of the

34. *Classical Age*, p. 86
35. Gnoli, R., *Op. cit.* Nos. XXIV and XXVII
36. Regmi, D. R., *Op. cit* p. 94

new era these dates correspond to the year 41-46. Udayadeva finds mention as a *yuvarāja* in the inscription of Aṁśuvarmā of the year 39 (A.D. 613) when Śivadeva was still living. We find last mention of Aṁśuvarmā in the year 45 (A.D. 619).[37] Most probably Udayadeva reigned until that time peacefully under the protection of Aṁśuvarmā. But soon after his death his younger brother[38] Dhruvdaeva dethroned him in about 620 A.D. We find inscriptions of Dhruvadeva dated in years 48 and 49 i.e. A.D. 622 and 623.

It is also possible that Udayadeva was killed and his son Narendradeva was compelled to leave the country for at least 20 years to come.

Thus between Udayadeva and his son Narendradeva there ruled Dhruvadeva and Bhīmārjunadeva from A.D. 620 A.D. to 640-41. These two kings were assisted by the successors of Aṁśuvarmā, Jushṇugupta and Viṣṇugupta. Either these two were a party with Dhruvadeva and Bhīmārjunadeva or they were neutral in the royal struggle. In either cases they had to face the wrath of Narendradradeva who at the time of his raid not only demolished the old ancestral Licchavi palace Mānagṛiha but also abolished his institution of second parallel royalty.

Afer Narendradeva the Licchavi history is clear upto Jayadeva II who was his grandson and the son of Śivadeva II.

Licchavi coins

Somehow or the other the Licchavi kings did not issue the coins in their name. We find mention of only two kings on the Licchavi coins, i.e. Mānadeva and Gaṇa (Guna) deva. Mānadeva was the first Licchavi king who started the tradition of writing inscription on stone etc., and, Gaṇādeva was the

37. Gnoli, R., *Op. cit.* No. XLVIII

38. cf. *Classical Age*, pp. 136-37 'Chinese sources give us some interesting information about him. They tell us that the father of Narendradeva i.e. Udayadeva, was removed from the throne by his younger brother. Narendradeva fled to Tibet and with the help of the Tibetan king recovered his paternal throne'.

father of Śivadeva I. The legends on both the type of coins is significant. These are *Manānka* and *Gunānka*, i.e. the seal of Māna (deva) and the seal of Guṇa (deva). We cannot take Mānāṇka and Guṇāṅka as personal epithets of these kings because in that case it should have been in nominative as it is in the class II silver coins of Chandragupta II of Gupta dynasty.[39] On the other hand we know definitely that the names of these kings were Mānadeva and Guṇa (Gaṇa) deva respectively. In that case *aṅka* should only mean the seal or the *Lāñcchana*. It appears that these two types of coins were commemorative in nature. It is mysterious that out of about sixteen Licchavi kings we find coins in the name ot only two kings. The other fact that increases the mystery is that we find coins issued in the names of secondary rulers like Aṁśuvarmā and Jiṣṇugupta etc. which led the scholars to speculate about their separate status or their independent nature. The third thing which strikes the scholars is the abundance and vast variety of Paśupati coins. So far no satisfactory explanation has come to light of these anomalies consequently the history of this period remains unexplained and confused.

It appears that the Licchavi rulers of Nepal for some reason or the other were abstaining themselves from issuing coins in their own names. It may be because of some supersitition or because the kingdom was dedicated to Lorg Paśupati. The latter reason seems to be the primary one and the first as second ary. A reference to the inscriptions issued under the advice of Aṁśuvarmā without the mention of the ruling king will show that they never fail to mention the words '*bhagavatapaśupati Bhaṭṭāraka pādānudhyato*'[40] or *pādānugrahito*'.[41] Aṁśuvarmā successors Jishṇugupta and Viṣṇugupta, also though mention the name of the ruling Licchavi king, always adopted this formula. These inscriptions of the Licchavi period show that *Bhaṭṭāraka* was the title

39. cf. Altekar, A. S., *Coinage of the Gupta Empire*, p. 154
40. Gnoli, R., *Op. cit.*, Nos. XXXV and XLIII
41. *Ibid.* Nos. XXXVI—XXXIX and LI—XLII & XLIV

reserved for the supreme ruler. We have already noted that *mahārājādhirāja* was not the title for the supreme ruler because Śivadeva conferred this title to his *Sāmanta* Aṁśuvarmā[13]. Thus there were, perhaps, two supreme rulers in Ancient Nepal, one the God Paśupati and the other his incarnation in the form of the Licchavi king. Even during our times the king in Nepal is regarded the incarnation of god Paśupati, and until the great revolution of 1950 he was an object of worship only and had little say in the administration. The point we want to emphasise in that during the Licchavi period the king was regarded the incarnation of god Paśupati or the kingdom was dedicated to the god; king was ruling on his behalf. If we understand this we can explain the vast variety and types of Paśupati coins.

During first few generations the Licchavi kings did not feel the necessity of issuing their own currency. Perhaps the need was not felt because of the undeveloped economy. But in the last quarter of the sixth century A.D., in the time of Śivadeva I, Nepal was perhaps having increased trade intercourse with India on the one hand and with Tibet and China on the other. This compelled the rulers of Nepal to issue their own coinage.

We cannot be sure as to who was the first ruler of Nepal to introduce coinage there. On stylistic grounds the Mānāṅka[43] coins are the earliest and they are nearer to the Gupta gold coins. The goddess on the reverse of this Mānāṅka coin seems to be a degenerated imitation of the reverse of a gold coin of Samudragupta.[44] Similarly one of the Paśupati coins bears a 'vase of flowers with streamers' on the reverse resembles the *loṭā* appearing on copper coins of Chandragupta II.[45] Furthermore the seated figures on the Licchavi coins

42. *Ibid*, No. XXXIII
43. *Walsh*, p. 1 No. 1
44. *JNSI* Vol. XXXII, pt. II, pl. VIII. No. 9
45. *Walsh*, pl. 1 No. 10page 678

also bear a close resemblance to those on the Gupta coins. These are enough to suggest the source of origin of Nepal coins of the Licchavi period. It will appear more reasonable if we keep in mind the time of these coins. The suggestions of their origin from Kushana or Yaudheya coins are less likely.

The Mānāṅka coin illustrated by Walsh[46] is a class in itself. There are some other *Mānāṅka* coins illustrated by S.M. Joshi[47] which. however, do not appear so much different from other coins of the period. The goddess seated on the reverse of one of these coins[48] does not seem much different from that on the Vaiśravaṇa coin or Guṇāṅka coins. There are some indications which show that these coins can be linked together. The figure of the cow on the Kāmadohi coin[49] of Aṁśuvarmā closely reremble to that on the Vaiśravaṇa coin[50]. In the same way the figure of lion on the mānāṅka[51] coin also resembles the lion one of the Aṁśuvarmā's[52] coins' The seated figures and the cow figures on all Paśupati coins can also be studied with this view point to find out that there cannot be a difference of more than a century among all these coins.

Mr. D. W. MacDowall has dọne a study of these coins on the basis of their weight standard. According to his observations 'the differences in weight between the groups is due entirely to a series of successive reductions in the weight standard. The heaviest coins are those of Aṁśuvarman which are struck to a standard of 11.14 gms. Those of Mānāṅka have a closely similar but slightly lower standard of 11.13 gms. Coins of Guṇāṅka fall into two groups, one

46. *Ibid*, pl. 1 No. 1
47. His plate page 5 Nos. 1—4 and plate page 6 No. 1
48. *Ibid*. Plate page 6 No. 1
49. *Walsh*, pl. II, No. 2
50. *Ibid*. pl. II. No. 1
51. *Ibid*. pl. II, No. 6
52. *Ibid*. pl. II, No. 4

at 12 gms and the other ranging between 7 and 10. This second group is far too heavy to be a fractional denomination and is clearly the result of a deliberate reduction in the weight standard. Coins with the name of Paśupati range from 3 to 10 gms.; but even in this group all the coins seem to have been intended as a single denomination and not as fractional'.[53]

MacDowall does not want to part with the belief that Nepal coinage was direct inheritor of the Kushāṇa coinage. He observes that 'the weight standard of coins of Aṁśuvarman (11-14 gms) seems to be derived ultimately from that of the main Kushāṇa copper denomination which Kanishka struck at between 16 and 17 gms.. and which Huvishka struck at 15-16 gms. in the earlier part of his reign'[54] He fails to apply the principle of weight reduction to connect the two sets coins i.e. Kushāṇa copper coins and the Licchavi coins. This reductions in weight was to adjust the trade and commerce relations. It is in most cases gradual. The gap of time between the two sets can well explain the reduction in weight from 11-16 gms. to 11-14 gms in the time of Aṁśuvarmā, i.e. late 6th century A.D. or the beginning of 7th century. It is most unlikely that 'Aṁśuvarman's coins would be struck to a standard 2-3 gms lighter to make them approximately equal in weight to any worn specimen of kanishka and Huvishka that may still have been in circulation.[55]

Thus it seems proper to think that it was during the time of the Licchavi king Sivadeva I and his Sāmanta, Mahārājādhirāja Aṁśuvarmā a necessity of issuing currency was felt in Nepal for the first time. According to Mac Dowell's frequency tables[56] the mean standard of and also the earliest ones are one Vaiśraveṇa, three Aṁśuvarma A. and two

53. *JNSI*, Vol. XXI, pl. I. p. 39
54. *Ibid.* p. 40
55. *Ibid.*
56. *Ibid.* pl. II, No. 1

Mānāṅka coins in 14 gms standard. In the 13 gms standard fall one Aṁśuvarman A, three Amsuvarman C, nine Mānāṅka and one Guṇāṅka A coins. In 12 gms standard there are two Aṁśuvarman A, two Aṁśuvarman B, four Aṁśuvarman C, eight Mānāṅk and three Guṇāṅka A coins. These can be regarded as the best representative weight groups of the time of Aṁśuvarmā. Thus Mānāṅka and Guṇāṅka coins are in all probability commemorative issues in the time of Aṁśuvarmā i.e. Śivadeva I. The Vaiśravaṇa coins may be taken to represent the present King Śivadeva I who was ruling over Nepal at that time. Aṁśuvarma's coins fall in 11, 10 and 9 gms, standard groups also which include Mānāṅka and Vaiśravaṇa types.

This is a unique example where the main line of kings are never mentioned by name in their coinage and on the other hand the secondary administrators found place on them by name. Perhaps the coinage was not so strictly associated with royalty in that time. The Vākāṭakas in Central India never issued coins where as their northern contemporaries, the Guptas, issued currency in abundance. But it may appear difficut to believe that those who appear on coins were not the primary or supreme rulers of the country and supreme monarch fails to mention his name.

The mention of the title *mahārājādhirāja* in the inscrip tion for his Sāmantā Aṁśurvarmā by the Supreme king Sivadeva I and appearance of this title on the cions associated with his personal name makes one to think shat perhaps the former never deserted the latter. It seems that during the old age of the king Aṁśuvarmā was granted the power to issue coins in his own name. There are reasons to believe this. The inscriptions issued in his own name from Kailāśakūṭa bhavana Aṁśuvarmā never styles himself as *bhaṭṭārakamahārāja* which was the title of the Licchvi kings throughout. He always styles himself as mahāsāmanta. Secondly, though he does not name the ruling king in these inscriptisns he very often names the crown prince Udayadeve as *dūtaka*. From the later inscriptions and Chinese tradition we can infer that this Udayadeva can be no other person than the father of Narendradeva the Licchavi king. Thirdly, the use of new era in all probability was to commemorate the event of the accession of his lord Sivadeva I to the throne. This was perhaps to show his gratitued and loyalty to the king who was not only his lord but relative also 57. As the most talented personality of his time Aṁśuvarmā wished to contribute his share by establishing some traditions for his king and country. These were the currency and the era. Both the traditions were new to the country but he lived long enough to get these firmly footed. Both these traditions were continued by the successive rulers. The new era was carried over by Narendra deva also who was so revengeful that he not only demolished the old Māngraha, the royal palace and lived for some time in the Kailāśakūṭa-bhavana but also abolished the institution of secondary royalty. Had the era been established as a result of revolt on the part of Aṁśuvarm, as it is presumed, it could never had been used by the successors of Sivadeva I. In all probability the relations between Sivadeva and Aṁśuvarmā never strained and the administration passed over from Aṁśuvarmā to Jiṣṇugupta very peacefully. The way Aṁśuvarmā finds mention in the inscription of the time of Dhruvadeva[58] and Jiṣṇugupta in the year 48 suggests very cordial relations. This never happens when the change of power take place by force or by way of revolt.

All these arguments only support the fact that relations between Sivadeva I and his Sāmanta Aṁśuvarmā were cordial and hit the theories of a separate kingdom of the latter. But perhaps no satisfactory explanation can be given to justify the issue of coins in their own name by

57. *Ibid*. pl. II, No. 6
58. *JNSI*, Vol. XXI, pl. I, p. 39

Aṁśuvarmā and his son and successor Jiṣṇugupta who were not rulers of the country, though the latter is known through only one coin to his credit, But as the established traditions were existing in his part of the world, including India, during those days coinage was not so firmly attached with royalty. There are several kings and some dynasties in India who never cared to issue coinage. Perhaps the Licchavis also did not attach much importance to this. But when such a necessity was felt and enthusiast Aṁśuvarmā pressed the matter he was perhaps granted permission to issue coins. However the indigenous coinage was introduced in Nepal and at first it was in the name of, as the analysis of Mac Dowell goes, Vaiśravaṇa. Then some coins were also issued to commemorate some past Licchavi king like Mānadeva and Gaṇadeva. But the main bulk of the coinage was issued in the time of Sivadeva I in the names of Paśupati, Mānadeva, Caṇadeva and Amśuvarma. Though the Paśupati coins were started during the reign of Sivadeva I under the inspiration of Aṁśuvarmā these were continued throughout the reign period of the Licchavis. This is evident from the frequency Tables of Mac Dowell[59] as their weight standard ranges from 11 gms to 3 gms.

59. *JNSI, Op. cit.* pp. 52-53

XVII

THE COINAGE OF NEPAL.

BY E. H. WALSH.

THE coins which are dealt with in the present paper fall under three divisions. *First*, the coins of the Early Licchavi Sūryavaṁśī dynasty, whose capital was at Mānagṛha, the present Kāṭhmāṇḍū, and those of the Ṭhākurī dynasty who were ruling at the same time over the western portion of Nepal, with their palace at Kailāśa-kūṭabhavana, situated in another part of the same city.[1] *Second*, the coins of the three Newār Malla dynasties, who reigned contemporaneously over the three kingdoms of Bhātgāon, Kāṭhmāṇḍū, and Pātan, or Lalitāpur. *Third*, the Gorkhā dynasty, founded on the conquest of Nepal by Pṛthvī Nārāyaṇa in 1768 A.D., and which continues to the present time.

Several of the coins now illustrated have appeared previously. The early coins, of the Sūryavaṁśī dynasty of Licchavi kings and of the Ṭhākurī dynasties (Plate I), have been described by Professor Bendall,[2] and have been described and illustrated in Cunningham's "Coins of Ancient India,"[3] and by Mr. V. Smith and Dr. Hoernl

[1] Fleet: "Early Chronology of Nepal," in the *Indian Antiquary*, vol. xiv, p. 350; and "The Early Gupta Inscriptions," *Corpus Inscriptionum Indicarum*, vol. iii, appendix, p. 189.

[2] "On some Nepalese Coins in the Library of the German Oriental Society": *Zeitschrift der Deutschen Morgenländischen Gesellschaft*, 1882 vol. xxxvi, p. 651.

[3] Sir A. Cunningham: "Coins of Ancient India," 1891, pl. xiii.

in the Proceedings of the Asiatic Society of Bengal,[1] but apart from the fact that some further varieties are now figured, the coins of these earlier dynasties, which have been already figured, have been included in the present paper so as to bring together what has been written on the subject, and because the subsequent silver coinage of the Newār Malla dynasty, though differing from them entirely in character, shows its continuity by the adoption of many of their symbols.

Of the seventy Malla coins shown on Plates II to VI, eight are illustrated by Marsden[2] and seven in the recent "Catalogue of Coins in the Indian Museum, Calcutta,"[3] by Mr. Vincent Smith, but the remaining fifty-five are, as far as I know, now illustrated for the first time. In the case of the coins of the present Gorkhā dynasty, shown on Plate VII, five have been illustrated by Marsden, and one, amongst those given in the recent Catalogue of Coins in the India Museum. But the other seven, I believe, have not before been illustrated.

The coins shown, of the Sūryavaṁśī and Thākurī dynasties, are in the British Museum; as are also those of the present Gorkhā dynasty. The coins of the Malla dynasties are partly from my own collection and partly from those in the British Museum. The coins from the British Museum are in each case noted in the list. The square double mohar of Pratāpa Malla (Pl. II, Fig. 14) is in the collection of Dr. Hoernle, who has kindly allowed me to reproduce it.

I have to thank the authorities of the British Museum

[1] Proceedings Asiatic Society of Bengal for May, 1887.

[2] Marsden: "Numismata Orientalia" (1825), pl. xlix; viz., Pl. II, Fig. 4 = Marsden MCXXII: Pl. II, Fig. 7 = MCXXIII; Pl. III, Fig. 8 = MCXX; Pl. IV, Fig. 2 = MCX, Fig. 3 = MCXI, Fig. 4 = MCXII, Fig. 7 = MCXIII, and Fig. 8 = MCXV.

[3] Vincent A. Smith, "Catalogue of Coins in the Indian Museum, Calcutta" (1906), vol. i, pl. xxviii; Marsden, op. cit., pl. i.

for allowing me to have casts from their coins of the thirteen early coins, figured on Plate I, as also of fourteen of the coins of the Newār Malla kings, which are shown on Plates II to VI as follows: Pl. II, Figs. 1 and 11; Pl. III, Fig. 3; Pl. IV, Figs. 1, 3, 4, 7, 8, 9, 10, 12, and 13; Pl. V, Fig. 7; Pl. VI, Fig. 9; and the thirteen coins of the present Gorkhā dynasty given on Plate VII; and to thank Dr. Hoernle for letting me have a cast of the square double mohar of Pratāpa Malla, in his collection (Pl. II, Fig. 14). The remaining fifty-one coins of the Newār Malla kings, forming Plates II to VI, are from my own collection.

As already noted, the coinage of Nepal falls under three main divisions. *First*, the early coins of the contemporaneous dynasty of Sūryavaṁśī Licchavi kings, whose capital was at Kailāśakūṭa,[1] and of Thākurī kings with an adjacent palace at Mānagṛha; *second*, those of the Malla dynasty of Newār kings which commenced with the conquest of the country by Jayasthiti Malla in 1380 A.D., and whose coinage commenced in 1556 A.D. and continued until the Gorkhā conquest; and *third*, those of the Gorkhā dynasty founded by Pṛthvī Nārāyaṇa Sāha's conquest of the country in 1768 A.D., and which continues to the present-time. The second period of the Newār kings also falls into three subdivisions; namely, the kingdoms of Bhātgāon and Kāṭhmāṇḍū into which the kingdom was divided by Yaksha Malla on his death *circ.* 1460 A.D., and the kingdom of Pātan or Lalitāpur, which was divided from that of Kāṭhmāṇḍū during the reign of Śivadeva, at the beginning on the seventeenth century.

The present kingdom of Nepal dates only from the Gorkhā conquest of Pṛthvī Nārāyaṇa in 1768. The

[1] Fleet, "Early Chronology of Nepal": *Indian Antiquary*, vol. xiv, p. 350.

kingdom of Nepal, to which the earlier coins and those of the Newār Malla dynasties belong, was practically the small area comprised in the Nepal Valley and the mountains which surround it. The valley itself is comparatively level at an elevation of about 4,500 feet, the bed of a former lake, and its extent is about twenty miles from east to west, and fifteen from north to south, though both length and breadth vary considerably owing to the spurs running down from the mountains. Within this area too, and within a few miles of each other,[1] were Bhātgāon, Kāṭhmāṇḍū, and Pātan, the capitals of their respective Malla kingdoms, and also the earlier Licchavi capital of Mānagṛha, and jointly the capital of the Ṭhākurī kings with its palace of Kailāśakūṭa, which, as all their coins come from the immediate neighbourhood of Pātan and Kāṭhmāṇḍū, and their inscriptions are found in the immediate vicinity of Kāṭhmāṇḍū, probably occupied the same or an adjacent site.[2]

Nepal in this restricted sense formed part of the empire of Asoka, but had ceased to form part of that of Samudra Gupta in the fourth century A.D. About 640 A.D. it seemed to have been subject to Harsha Vardhana, as his era, which dated from 606–7 A.D., is found on inscriptions in the country at that time.[3] His suzerainty, however, lasted only a few years, and at the time of his death, in 648 A.D., Nepal was a dependency of Tibet, which it continued to be until 880 A.D., when the institution of the Newār Era shows that the Newār kingdom had then succeeded in throwing off the Tibetan suzerainty, and had become an independent kingdom.

[1] Pātan is only two miles south-east of Kāṭhmāṇḍū, and Bhātgāon nine miles to the east of it and eight miles from Pātan.

[2] Fleet, "The Early Gupta Inscriptions": *Corpus Inscriptionum Indicarum*, vol. iii, Appendix, p. 189.

[3] Fleet, "Inscriptions of the Early Gupta Kings and their Successors": *Corpus Inscriptionum Indicarum*, vol. iii, Appendix, p. 189.

The history of Nepal, as given in the native chronicles, commences with the creation of the world, but is chiefly concerned with gods and mythological personages, until the time of Ne Muni, from whom the country is said to derive its name. This sage, having come to Nepal from the south, persuaded the people that there would be no Kṣatria Rājas in the Kali Yuga, and installed as king one of the Goala settlers, who are said to have come into the country shortly before, with Kṛṣṇa.[1] There were eight kings of this first Gupta dynasty, when, as the last king, Yakṣa Gupta, had no issue, an Āhīr from the plains of Hindustan came and ruled over the country. This Āhīr dynasty continued for three generations, when the Kirātīs came from east and conquered the country. There were twenty-nine kings of the Kirātī dynasty, when they were conquered by the Somavaṁśīs, who ruled the country for five generations. The last of the Somavaṁśī kings, having no children, "appointed as his successor one Bhūmi-varman, a Kṣatria of the Solar race of Rājpūts of the Gautama gotra, who had been one of the followers of Śākya Siṁha Buddha of Kapilavastu, and had remained in Nepal after his departure."[2] The Vaṁśāvalī gives the names of thirty-one kings of the Sūryavaṁśī dynasty, the sixteenth of whom, Śiva Deva, is the first whose date can be fixed. His date has been fixed from his inscriptions at 635 A.D.; as also that of Aṁśu-varman, Śiva Deva's minister, who founded the contemporary dynasty of Thākurī kings The subsequent kings of these dynasties, with their dates as fixed from inscriptions, are given by Dr. Fleet[3] as follows, the serial number being that which they occupy in the Vaṁśāvalī:—

[1] Wright: "History of Nepal," p. 108.

[2] Wright, op. cit., p. 114.

[3] Fleet: *Corpus Inscriptionum Indicarum*, vol. iii, p. 178.

Licchavi Sūryavaṁśī Dynasty.			Thākurī Dynasty.		
	A.D.			A.D.	
16	635	Śivadeva.	1	635	Aṁśuvarman.
17	654	Dhruvadeva.		654	Jisnu Gupta.
18		Vṛiṣhadeva.			Udayadeva.
19		Śānkaradeva.			Narendradeva
20		Dharmadeva.		725	Śivadeva II.
21	705	Mānadeva.	12	751	Jayadeva II.
22	733	Mahīdeva.			
23	754	Vasantasena.			

The fact that Aṁśu-varman was reigning between 640 A.D. and 650 A.D. is also proved by the narrative of the Chinese pilgrim Hiuen Tsang.

The succeeding names of the Licchavi dynasty are given in the Vaṁśāvalī as follows:—[1]

24. Udayadeva.
25. Mānadeva.
26. Guṇakāmadeva-varman.
27. Śivadeva-varman.
28. Narendradeva-varman.
29. Bhīmadeva.
30. Viṣṇudeva-varman.
31. Viṣvadeva-varman.

The names of the Ṭhākurī dynasty as given in the Vaṁśāvalī differ altogether from those given above for that dynasty. Professor Sylvain Lévi, however, assigns an earlier date to the above Licchavi kings. He considers that there is not sufficient evidence to show that they were subject to Samudra Gupta, but that the word *pratyanta* ('frontier states'), amongst which Nepal is included, in the panegyric of Samudra Gupta has been misunderstood, and means, not a subject state, but an

[1] Wright: "History of Nepal," p. 313.

independent state forming the boundary of the empire. He therefore considers that the dates in their inscriptions are either in a Licchavi era of their own, which commenced in 113 A.D., or are in the Śāka era, and fixes the date of Mānadeva as between 497 and 524 A.D. on the former hypothesis, or between 464 and 491 A.D. on the latter, and considers that in his time the kingdom was not partitioned.[1]

At the time when the coinage of Nepal commences, there were, thus, reigning from a joint capital at Kāṭhmāṇḍū a dynasty of Licchavi kings, who are styled in their inscriptions *Licchavikula* and in the native chronicles *Sūryavaṁśa*, who used the Gupta era, reigning over the eastern portion of the country, and of Ṭhākurī kings, who used the Harsha era, reigning from a joint capital over the western portion.[2]

The coins of the first period have been described by Sir A. Cunningham in "Coins of Ancient India";[3] by Professor Bendall, who has described the specimens of these coins in the library of the German Oriental Society;[4] and by Mr. V. Smith and Dr. Hoernle, who have described specimens of these coins in the Proceedings of the Asiatic Society of Bengal.[5]

A coin of the same type as that shown on Pl. I, Fig. 5, is figured by Professor Rapson in his "Indian Coins,"[6] and a specimen of the type given in Pl. I, Fig. 10, is figured in "The New Catalogue of Coins in the Indian Museum, Calcutta" (pl. xxviii, fig. 1). For convenience of

[1] Sylvain Lévi: "Le Népal," pp. 113–116; Leroux, Paris, 1905.

[2] Fleet, op. cit., p. 190.

[3] Sir A. Cunningham: "Coins of Ancient India" (1891), p. 112 et seq., and pl. xiii.

[4] *Zeitschrift der Deutschen Morgenländischen Gesellschaft*, Leipzig, 1882, vol. xxxvi, p. 651.

[5] P.A.S.B. for May, 1887, and March, 1898.

[6] "Indian Coins," by E. J. Rapson: *Grundriss der Indo-Arischen Philologie und Altertumskunde*, vol. ii, p. 32, and pl. v, fig. 10.

reference I give below a Table showing the specimens of the early Nepal coins which have been previously described.[1]

These early coins are large copper pieces of varying weight, but with the exception of coins No. 1 (197 grains) and No. 6 (249 grains), they approximate to a standard of 1¼ paṇas, or 180 grains, the weight of the paṇa being 144 grains.[2] As noted by Sir A. Cunningham

[1] Table for reference to early Nepal coins previously described :—

Plate I.	Cunningham, "Coins of Ancient India."	Prof. Bendall.	V. Smith and Dr. Hoernle.	
Figure. 1	Coin No. 1	"Alte Schrift," Coin Nos. 2, 3, 4, and 5.	III (a), (b), and (c).	Prof. Rapson, "Indian Coins," pl. i, fig. 10.
2	A variety of coin No. 2.			
3	2			
4	3	1		
5	4	6, 10	II (a) and (b).	
6	5		I	
7	6	7, 8, 9, 11, and 12.	IV (a) and (b).	
8	7			
9	8			
Not figured, coin No. 10.	9 Obv. as pl. i, fig. 9; Rev. as pl. i, fig. 8.			
10	10 11 Similar, with bull to l.	"Neuere Schrift," Nos. 1, 2, and 3.		V. Smith, C.C.I.M.C., pl. xxviii, fig. 1.
11	12 13 Similar, no legend.			
12	15			
13	14			

[2] The Indian *paṇa*, 'handful,' derived from *pāṇi*, 'the hand,' "was a handful of cowrie shells usually reckoned at 80. This term *paṇ* is still used in Bengal, where a *paṇ* of cowrie shells consists of 20 gaṇḍas, or '20 fours' of cowries. By repeated trials I have found that 80 cowries form a very fair average handful. But the *paṇa* was also a copper coin of 80 rati seeds in weight (144 grains) and 80 cowries in value" (Cunningham, C.A.I., p. 1).

and Professor Rapson,[1] they bear a resemblance to the second class of Yaudeya coins, which is probably due to a common origin from the coins of the Kuṣāṇas. Their symbols of the standing humped bull and the standing lion with its tail curled over its back are also found on the Rajañya coins of the second or first century B.C.[2] The standing bull and standing lion on two of those coins are exactly the same as on the Nepal coins. The conclusion that the Nepal coinage was derived from that of the Kuṣāṇas is borne out by the fact that Kuṣāṇa coins have been dug up in the neighbourhood of Kāṭhmāṇḍū, which would seem to show that these coins were either current in Nepal in early times, being brought by merchants, or were brought by pilgrims. I have two coins of Wema Kadphises (85–120 A.D.) and one of Kanishka (120–150 A.D.), which were dug up at Kāṭhmāṇḍū, which were sent me by Colonel Pears when resident in Nepal. The seated figure of a deity on a lotus-seat, and also the seated figure of a deity or king on a throne with one leg hanging down, were also probably copied from the Kuṣāṇa coinage. In some coins of Huvishka[3] the seated figure is so like that on Mānāṅka's coin (Pl. I, Fig. 1) as to at once suggest the connection. The seated figure of the deity or king with one leg hanging down, and the trident on long straight shaft with battle-axe to left, as on coins of Paśupati (Pl. I, Fig. 2), also have their prototypes in the Kuṣāṇa coins of Kadphises II[4] and of Huvishka, the humped bull standing by itself in coins of Kadphises I[5] and the elephant in coins of Huvishka, though with a rider on its back. The elaborate symbol of a trident on the reverse of the coin of Jiṣṇu Gupta, resembling the

[1] E. J. Rapson, op. cit., p. 32.

[2] "Catalogue of Coins in Indian Museum, Calcutta," 1906, vol. i, p. 179, pl. xxi, figs. 11 and 12.

[3] C.C.I.M.C., vol. i, p. 82, serial 47, and pl. xiii, fig. 5.

[4] Ibid., p. 68, serial 5, and pl. xi, fig. 6.

[5] Ibid., p. 67, serial 17, and pl. xi, fig. 4.

Florentine Giglia, appears to be a form of the "*nandipada triśula*," the two hoofs of the bull *Nandi* forming the pedestal at its base. A simple design, the parts of which are essentially the same though unelaborately formed, but in which the two hoofs clearly appear, occurs on a coin of Raja Kumuda Sena,[1] one of the early kings of Ayodhya (between 150 B.C. to 100 A.D.), with a standing bull on the reverse, similar to the bull on the Nepal coins. The seated figures also bear a close resemblance to those on the Gupta coins. The vase of flowers with streamers which figures on the coins of Paśupati (Pl. I, Figs. 12 and 13) occurs on copper coins of Chandra Gupta II (about 375–413 A.D.), where it bears the same shape as that of the ordinary brass *lota*, and the resemblance suggests that the Nepal coin was copied from that coin.

The names which appear on the coins are as follows :—

MĀNĀṄKA. (Coin No. 1; Pl. I, Fig. 1.)

This name does not occur in the list of kings given in the Vaṁśāvalī. But it would appear to be the same as Mānadeva, whose date, as already noted, is given by Dr. Fleet as 705 A.D., and by Professor Lévi as either 497 A.D. or 464 A.D. Professor Bendall[2] thought that it was probably another namé, or *biruda*, of Aṁśu-varman. But he based this opinion on the supposition that the legend on the obverse is *Śrī Bhaginī*, and suggested that the explanation of the legend is to be found in inscription No. 7 of the series of inscriptions published in *The Indian Antiquary*, vol. ix, p. 171, in which King Aṁśu-varman proclaims that his sister (*Bhaginī*) Bhogadevī has dedicated a linga to the temple of Paśupati. The legend on the obverse, however, is clearly not *Bhaginī*, but *Bhoginī*, 'the enjoyable one,' which probably applies to the goddess

[1] C.C.I.M.C., vol. i, p. 150, serial 14, and pl. xix, fig. 15.

[2] *Zeitschrift der Deutschen Morgenländischen Gesellschaft*, vol. xxxvi, p. 651.

seated on the lotus, as Dr. Hoernle supposes.[1] Professor Sylvain Lévi[2] points out that the term *Bhoginī* was used for the wives of kings other than the principal wife, the Mahisī, but thinks it unlikely that such a title would be used as the name of a person, or placed on a coin, and also considers that it is the name of the goddess. In any case there appears to be no sufficient reason to suppose it to be a coin of Aṁśu-varman's, or Mānāṅka to be his *biruda*. Dr. Hoernle reads Mānaṅka, 'the Māna-marked,' as a *biruda* of Mānadeva, 'the lord of Māna,' a name which in both cases was taken by him owing to his belonging to the family who ruled from the palace of Mānagṛha. Professor Lévi,[3] on the other hand, takes the word to apply to the coin 'bearing the mark of Māna,' viz. Mānadeva.

GUṆĀṄKA. (Coin No. 2; Pl. I, Figs. 2 and 3.)

('Bearing the mark of Guṇa.') This would appear to be a coin of Gunakāmadeva, who, according to the Vaṁśāvalī, was the twenty-sixth king of the Licchavi dynasty. Professor Lévi reads Guṇāṅka (similarly to Mānāṅka) as meaning money bearing the mark of Guṇa (-kāmadeva). The coins of this name bear a seated goddess on the obverse and an elephant on the reverse. The coin No. 2 is the only type of these Early Nepal coins which is not surrounded with the characteristic of dots, but has a plain convex band in place of it.

VAIŚRAVAṆA. (Coin No. 4; Pl. I, Fig. 4.)

This name does not occur in the list of kings given in the Vaṁśāvalī. Cunningham suggests that as the name is a patronymic of Kuvera it might possibly be a coin of Kuvera Deva, the ninth king of the Sūryavaṁśī dynasty. But, as he observes, this would place the date of the coin

[1] P.A.S.B. for March, 1888. [2] "Le Népal," vol. ii, p. 107.
[3] "Mānāṅka: (monnaie) à la marque de Māna:" Le Népal, vol. ii, p. 106.

too early, as it is of the same nature as the others, and the Gupta characters of the inscription are of the same date. It is probably, therefore, the name of a god, as in the case of the coins of Paśupata, and its date cannot be fixed. These coins bear a seated figure on the obverse and the divine cow "Kāmadehi" (or Kāmadhenu) on the reverse, as in the coins of Aṁśu-varman.

Kāmadhenu is connected with the legendary history of Nepal, as given in the Vaṁśāvalī, in the following manner :—Maheśvar appeared in the shape of a deer in a grove near Kāṭhmāṇḍū, and disclosed himself in the form of light which pervaded the seven firmaments above the earth and the seven firmaments below. On seeing this Brahmā went upwards to see how far the light extended, and Viṣṇu went downwards for the same purpose. Having returned from their journeys they met near a village on the hill south of Kāṭhmāṇḍū, and on comparing notes Viṣṇu said that he was not able to find the limit to which the light extended, whilst Brahmā declared that he had gone beyond it. Viṣṇu then called for witnesses, and Brahmā produced Kāmadhenu, who on being asked to declare the truth corroborated Brahmā's assertion with her mouth, whilst she shook her tail by way of denying it. Viṣṇu then, seeing what was the truth, uttered a curse on Brahmā, to the effect that his image should nowhere be worshipped, and on Kāmadhenu, that her mouth should be impure, but her tail sacred. Having done this, he remained in that place with the cow, but Brahmā disappeared.[1]

AṀŚU-VARMAN. (Coins Nos. 5–7 ; Pl. I, Figs. 5–7.)

This king, who was the founder of the Ṭhākurī dynasty, reigned from 635 to 654 A.D. His coins bear on the obverse a winged lion with raised paw. The lion on his coins differs from that on Mānāṅka's coin in being winged, but

[1] Wright, p. 82.

there is an unwinged lion similar to Mānāṅka's on the obverse of one type of his coins (Fig. 7). On the obverse of another type of his coins (Fig. 5) is the divine cow "Kāmadehi," and on another (Fig. 6) is the title, Mahārājādhirājasya, round a central sun.

JIṢṆU GUPTA. (Coin No. 8; Pl. I, Fig. 8.)

This king was the son and successor of Aṁśu-varman. His date is also fixed, by inscriptions, at 654 A.D., which is corroborated by the narrative of Hiuen Tsang. His coin bears a winged bull with raised paw on the obverse, but it differs from the lion on his father's coins in having the tail hanging down and not curled over the back. The reverse is an elaborately ornamental form of the trident.

PAŚUPATI. (Coins Nos 9–20; Pl. I, Figs. 9–13.)

There is nothing to fix the date of these coins. They are of six distinct types, four of which are shown on the Plate. On the obverses are a recumbent bull, a standing bull with crescent, a trident with an axe attached to its shaft; on the reverse of these coins are various forms of a sun with rays. There is also another type (Fig. 12) with a seated crowned figure, apparently a king, on the obverse, and a vase of flowers on the reverse, which resembles coins of the Guptas, and would appear to have been copied from them. There is also another type (coin No. 16; not illustrated) on the obverse of which is a recumbent bull, as in Pl. I. Fig 9, and on the reverse the ornamental form of "*nandipada triśula*" found on the reverse of Jiṣṇu Gupta's coin (Fig. 8). This is interesting, for as it appears to be the only coin of Paśupati bearing that reverse, whereas there are several examples of the other types, it suggests that the reverse of this coin, which is unusual for the Paśupati coins, was copied from that of Jiṣṇu Gupta, and thus shows that these coins are subsequent to his date.

The number of these early coins which have been found is not large. Cunningham[1] mentions that he obtained most of the coins which he describes from Colonel Warren, who collected them in Kashmir. According to his list there were about a hundred legible coins and thirty-seven that were unnamed. Cunningham himself also had twenty-three coins that came from Benares, and twenty which he obtained at Gaya by purchase in the Bazaar, or at Buddha Gaya in the small votive stūpas. The Gaya coins were, as he says, no doubt found by workpeople at Buddha Gaya, and were no doubt votive offerings of pilgrims from Nepal. The coins described by Mr. V. Smith and Dr. Hoernle were from a collection of forty coins obtained at Kāṭhmāṇḍū by Dr. Gimlette, the Residency surgeon.[2] Dr. Hoernle has a collection of eleven of these coins which he collected at Kāṭhmāṇḍū, and I have seven from Kāṭhmāndū. There are 106 of these coins in the British Museum, but some of them are from Cunningham's and Colonel Warren's collections, and are therefore included in the numbers already given. The number of specimens of each type of coin in the British Museum is given in the list of these coins.

Cunningham, writing in 1891, says: "The coins of Paśupati are by far the most numerous, as they form about half of the known specimens of the early Nepalese coinage. The coins of Aṁśuvarma form about one-fourth, and the remainder are nearly equally divided between Mānāṅka, Guṇāṅka, and Jiṣṇu Gupta."[3] To the latter should be added Vaiśravana.

[1] C.A.I., p. 114.

[2] Of these, a coin of Mānāṅka (Pl. I, Fig. 1) and the three coins of Aṁśu-varman (Pl. I, Figs. 5–7) were made over to the Asiatic Society of Bengal, and are now in the Indian Museum at Calcutta. There was only one specimen of Aṁśu-varman's coin (Pl. I, Fig. 6) amongst the lot. Three specimens of Mānāṅka and five of Aṁśu-varman, which were then retained by Mr. V. Smith, are now in the Bibliothèque Nationale, Paris (V. Smith, C.C.I.M.C.. vol. i, p. 283).

[3] C.A.I., p. 115.

I have not ascertained the number of these coins in the Bodleian Collection, or those in the Cambridge Museum, or the Museum of the Bibliothèque Nationale at Paris.

COINS OF THE MALLA DYNASTY OF NEWĀR KINGS.

The coinage of the Newār kings is of an entirely different character to the previous coins of Nepal already noticed. With the exception of one king of Kāṭhmāṇḍū, Jaya Prakāśa (1736 A.D.), who coined gold as well as silver, the coinage is entirely a silver coinage. It is based on a mohar of the weight of six māṣās, a broad bean used in India as a weight. Cunningham notes that the māṣā averages 14·6 grains,[1] and the weight of six māṣās is therefore 87·6 grains. The mohars, with the exception of lighter coins of one or two kings, vary in weight between 80 and 90 grains, and the fractional coins based on them show a corresponding variation in proportion. Half mohars, quarter mohars, eighth mohars, and in the case of one king, Jaya Prakāśa, a sixteenth of a mohar and a do-dām, or thirty-second part of a mohar, were also coined. The value of the mohar was eight annas, and two of them were equivalent to the Mogul rupee.

Although there is one specimen of a double mohar, the square coin of Pratāpa Malla, shown on Pl. II, Fig. 14, the fact that there are no other coins of this value, and that the square form does not occur again, leads to the conclusion that this specimen must have been a medal, or a *niṣār*. Kirkpatrick distinctly says that the *sicca*, or double mohar, "has been known in this country only since the time of Pṛthvi Nārāyaṇ." [2]

The Vaṁśāvali (Native Chronicle), translated in Wright's "History of Nepal," says that Ratna Malla (the first king of the separate kingdom of Kāṭhmāṇḍū), "having brought

[1] "Coins of Ancient India," p. 2.

[2] Kirkpatrick, op. cit., p. 217.

copper from Tāmbā Khani, introduced pice (*paisā*) into the currency instead of *sukichās*" (viz. quarter mohars, worth eight pice), but I have not heard of any copper coins of the Mallas, and the chronicle probably refers to the "dumpy pice," lumps of copper, which were used in Nepal, as, until recently, in India.[1]

The mohar was first coined by Mahendra Malla, King of Kāṭhmāṇḍū, who reigned in 1566 A.D. In the Vaṁśāvalī it is recorded that: "He went to Dihli with a present of a swan and hawks for the Emperor, who, being much pleased therewith, granted him permission to strike coin in his own name, in weight six mashas. He struck this coin and called it Mohar, and made it current in every part of his country." [2]

Professor Lévi thinks that this story of Mahendra Malla's visit to the Emperor of Delhi is open to suspicion; as the reign of Mahendra Malla fell between 1550 and 1570 A.D., when the throne of Delhi was violently shaken. Humayun had been defeated by the Afghan Sher Khān in 1539, and had fled from the country. Sher Shah's successors were weakened by internal wars. Humayun returned and took Delhi in 1555, and died six months after. His son Akbar was a minor, and did not exercise personal rule until the close of 1560, and then passed seven years in putting down the seditions which broke out in all parts.[3]

But, however this may be, what made it possible for Mahendra Malla to strike a silver coinage was the fact that he made a treaty with Tibet, by which he supplied the coinage of that country, and obtained from Tibet the silver for the purpose. This privilege, besides supplying Nepal with the silver for its own coinage, continued to be the source of an extensive annual revenue to Nepal,

[1] Wright: "History of Nepal" (1877), p. 203.
[2] Ibid., p. 207.
[3] Lévi: "Le Népal," vol. ii, p. 246.

from the royalty it obtained on the coins that were supplied from it for currency in Tibet.

This privilege of supplying the currency of Tibet was at any rate subsequently shared by the kingdom of Bhātgāon, and, in fact, became the monopoly of that kingdom; for the coin of Bhūpatīndra Malla of Bhātgāon (Pl. II, Fig. 3) was current in Tibet, and while the last coins of this early pattern, of Kāṭhmāṇḍū, are those of Pratāpa Malla, A.D. 1641, and of Pātan, those of Śrī Nivāsa, A.D. 1661, they continued to be coined by Bhātgāon up to the end of the Malla dynasty. The earliest examples of the Malla coinage of the three kingdoms respectively are that of Lakṣmīnara Siṁha of Kāṭhmāṇḍū, undated (Pl. II, Fig. 9); next, that of his successor, Pratāpa Malla, of date 1641 A.D. (Pl. II, Fig. 10); of Jagatprakāśa of Bhātgāon, of date 1642 A.D. (Pl. II, Fig. 1); and of Siddhi Narasiṁha of Pātan, of date 1631 A.D. (Pl. V, Fig. 1). These coins are all of the same design. This shows that the kingdom of Bhātgāon in its coinage, and subsequently, on its formation, the kingdom of Pātan, adopted the design which was probably adopted from the first by Jaya Mahendra Malla for the Tibetan coinage, and at the same time for the coinage of Nepal itself. It will thus be seen that although the Nepal-Tibet coinage was commenced by Jaya Mahendra about the year 1556, there are no examples of his coinage nor of that of his successors, Sadāśiva Malla, Śiva Deva, or Hariharasiṁha, the earliest being that of Lakṣmīnara Siṁha and his contemporaries Jagatprakāśa of Bhātgāon and Siddhi Narasiṁha of Pātan. Even these are earlier than any coin that I have come across in Tibet, where the earliest coin I have found is that of Bhūpatīndra Malla of Bhātgāon, of date 1696 (Pl. II, Fig. 3), and of that I have only found two specimens, and these were considered rarities.

Marsden notes that the Gorkhā king Pṛthvi Nārāyaṇa called in all the previous coinage of the Malla dynasties, so that even in his own reign it was difficult to obtain any of the money of his predecessors, but this would not account for the disappearance of only the coins of the earlier kings, while specimens of the later ones remain, nor for their disappearance in Tibet. Although the quantity coined at first was probably small, it is still difficult to account for this entire disappearance of the earlier coinage.

In a paper on the coinage of Tibet, which I read before the Asiatic Society of Bengal,[1] I suggested that the characters around the margin of these coins, which no Newār or Tibetan understands or can account for, might be intended for an imitation of the characters on the seal of the Dalai Lama, which they to some extent resemble. The Dalai Lama's seal is the official symbol of the Tibetan Government, for whose circulation they were intended, and I thought that for this reason it was not unlikely that the seal might be represented on a coin intended for the currency of Tibet.

At the time of reading the present paper, however, Professor Rapson pointed out that, if looked at upside down, they bear a close resemblance to the Arabic characters on the coins of the Mahomedan kings of Bengal. I think there is no doubt that he is right, and the resemblance to certain coins of Ghiyāṣ-ud-dīn Mahmūd Shāh, who was king of Bengal from 1526 to 1537 A.D., is so striking as to suggest that these particular coins were copied by Mahendra Malla for his mohar. I give below for comparison a copy of coins Nos. 147 and 149, in the Catalogue of the Coins of the Kings of Bengal in the British Museum, together with a copy of the coin of Lakṣminara Siṁha, the earliest of the coins of Kāṭhmāṇḍū, which is shown on Pl. II, Fig. 9:—

[1] E. H. C. Walsh, "The Coinage of Tibet": Memoirs A.S.B., vol. ii, No. 2, p. 11.

1 2 3

1. Coin No. 149, viewed upside down, of Ghiyās-ud-dīn Mahmūd Shāh, date 934 A.H. = 1527 A.D.[1]
2. Coin No. 147, of Ghiyās-ud-dīn Mahmūd Shāh, date 933 A.H. = 1526 A.D.
3. Coin of Laksmīnara Siṁha of Kāṭhmāṇḍū.

[1] "Catalogue of Indian Coins in the British Museum," by Stanley Lane Poole, 1885, p. 14.

KINGS OF BENGAL.

XLIX. *Ghiyās-ud-dīn Maḥmūd Shāh III.*

(Partial rule, A.H. 933–9 = A.D. 1526–32 ; A.H. 939–44 = A.D. 1532–37.)

No.	Mint and Date.	Description.
		Silver.
147	Nasratābād. 933	Obv. السلطان بن / السلطان غياث / الدنيا ◯ والدين / أبو المظفر محمود Rev. شاه السلطان / بن حسين شاه / السلطان ◯ خلد الله / ملكه وسلطانه ٩٣٣ / نصرتاباد In each centre, small circle— شاهى / بدر Plate vii. Æ. 1·05. Wt. 166.
149	Muhammad-ābād. 934	Same, but شاه transposed from beginning of rev. to end of obv. ; inscription differently arranged, and mint and date محمداباد ٩٣٤. Plate vii. I.O.C. Æ. 1·05

The resemblance of the Nepal coin to both the coins of Ghiyās-ud-dīn referred to is most striking, and especially to No. 149, from which the circle of dots round the margin of these coins would also seem to be copied. The territories of the Bengal kings were conterminous with Nepal, and their coins no doubt found their way into that country and were familiar there, which accounts for their being imitated by Mahendra Malla when he instituted his coinage.

The enclosure of the inscription within a square area, on these first Malla coins, was also probably copied from the coins of the Bengal kings, and occurs on the coins of Muhammad Shāh Ghāzi[1] = A.D. 1552–1554, and Ghiyās-ud-dīn Bahādur Shāh,[2] 1554–1560.

The following is an extract from the paper which I read before the Asiatic Society of Bengal on the Coinage of Tibet (Memoirs A.S.B., vol. ii, No. 2, pp. 11–23) :—

Kirkpatrick, in the account of his mission to the kingdom of Nepal in 1793, writes: "The silver eight-anna piece, now called Mohr and Adheeda, was formerly denominated Mehnder-Mulie,[3] after the Prince who first struck it, and by treaty established it in the neighbouring kingdom of Tibet; this prince would appear to have been one of the successors of Hur Sing Deo, and of the dynasty of Khatmanda, which city is said to have exclusively enjoyed for some time the privilege of supplying Tibet with coin, a privilege the more singular as it was from this very country that Nepal obtained her silver bullion. The origin of this practice is ordinarily referred to the superstitious reverence in which the valley of Nepal, and, more especially, the north-west parts of it (highl celebrated for their sanctity), has been wont to be held by the spiritual sovereigns of Tibet; but, whatever may have been the cause of it, there is not a doubt that the present Nepal Government made the departure of the Tibetans from ancient usage in this respect, the pretext for the war which it waged

[1] Catalogue of Indian Coins in the British Museum: "Kings of Bengal" 58, pl. vii, fig. 138.

[2] Ibid., p. 58, pl. vii, fig. 133.

[3] Mahendra Malla, 1566 A.D.

about four years ago against the confederated Lamas; as evidently appears from a memorial transmitted to me from Nepal on this subject, an extract of which is given in Appendix No. II.

"The Mehnder-Mulie exhibited anciently a representation of Lehassa on one side, and, on the reverse, the name, titles, and emblems of the reigning sovereign of Khatmandu. Since the conquest of Nepal by Purthi Narain, no allusion to Lehassa has been preserved, the Mohr bearing on one side the following inscription: Sri Sri Sri Run Behauder Shah Dewa, and, on the other, Sri Sri Goorknāth Sri Bhowāni, with the year of the Soka and certain emblems allusive to the Hindu superstition, as the sun, moon, Trisool, of Mahadeo, etc."[1]

With reference to this statement of Kirkpatrick's Professor Lévi[2] says that a coin figured in the *Missio Apostolica Thibetana*[3] simply bears on the obverse the effigy of the king, and on the reverse a horse standing towards the left and turning back his head. I have referred to this coin, which is figured on p. 202 of the *Missio Apostolica.* It is clearly a coin of the Yueh-ti, and is an imitation of the coins of the Indo-Scythians, and, allowing for its being a larger size and for elaborate drawing, is similar to a coin figured by Sir A. Cunningham on plate xiii of vol. ix of third series of the *Numismatic Chronicle.* As the *Missio Apostolica Thibetana* is not generally procurable, I give below a tracing of the coin referred to, together with Cunningham's coin which it resembles :—

[1] "An Account of the Kingdom of Nepal, being the substance of observations made during a mission to that country in the year 1793," by Col. Kirkpatrick, London, William Miller, 1811, pp. 217, 218.

[2] Lévi: "Le Népal," vol. ii, p. 247.

[3] "Missio Apostolica Thibetana Seraphica. Das is neue durch Päbstlichen Gewalt indem Grossen Thibetanische Reich. Von denem P.P. Capucineren aufgerichtete Mission und über Dolche von R. P. Francisco Horatio della Penna, etc." München, 1740.

1.

2.

FIG. 1. Tracing of coin given on p. 202, *Missio Apostolica Thibetana.*
FIG. 2. Yueh-ti coin, figured by Sir A. Cunningham.[1]

From the above, it is clear that the coin referred to is not the original Nepalese coinage for Tibet, and is not in fact a Tibetan coin at all. It appears at the foot of a plate of what purports to be an example of Tibetan writing ("Thibetaner Schrift"), but which is actually a Christian invocation and the Lord's Prayer, written in Hindi! This shows the value of the plate as regards the coin also, to which I do not find any reference in the text, and, as Orazio della Penna could not have made such a mistake as to show Hindi writing as an example of Tibetan, the whole plate has, I think, been edited into the book by the compilers, who evidently in Europe did not know what either the writing or the coin was, but thought them suitable material to illustrate an Oriental book.

The originally exclusive privilege of the Raja of Khāṭmāṇḍū to coin for Tibet, mentioned by Kirkpatrick, did not long continue,

[1] The coin is described as follows: "Pl. i, fig. 4, 0·5 in., AR., 28 gr. Rude copy of silver drachma. Diademed head of king to l. with moustaches. Native legend of five characters behind the head, as in No. 3. Rev.: Horse's head to l. with Greek letter κ. N.B.—These coins are very rare, but there are numbers of very rude copies in two different sizes."—*Numismatic Chronicle*, ser. III, vol. ix (1889), pl. xiii, fig. 4.

but was also shared by the kingdom of Bhātgāon, by the time of Bhūpatīndra Malla, whose coins were current in Tibet, where they are known as *angi drug-pa*, or 'number six,' from the last figure of their Newār date, 816; while those of Jaya Raṇajita Malla, the last king of Bhātgāon, are still current.

The reason for the discontinuance of this coinage was, that it became so debased under the later kings of Bhatgaon that when the Gorkhas conquered the country they would not continue coining coins for Tibet if they had to exchange at *par* with the debased coins then in circulation, and the dispute over this question was made the pretext of the war between Nepal and Tibet in 1792. Kirkpatrick publishes an "extract from a Memorial of the Court of Khatmāndū, relative to the origin of the War with Tibet," which gives a full account of the dispute. I give below the portion which relates to the coinage:—

"In ancient times there subsisted a close union between the Rajahs of Nepaul and Bhoat (i.e. Tibet); when the pure Mehnder-mulli of the coinage of the former country was the current money of the latter. During the respective reigns, however, of Rajah Jy Purkaush Mull, the sovereign of Nepal, and of Rajah Runjeet Mull, the ruler of Bhatgong, the Mehnder-mulli became much debased, the consequence of which was that at the period Nepal passed into the possession of the Goorkha, Bhoat was full of this base coin. The Maharajah (i.e. Pirthi Nerain) immediately put a stop to this improper practice, sending at the same time a friendly deputation to Bhoat for the purpose of stating the mischievous consequences that would ensue were it persisted in, and of engaging the Lamas to revert to the ancient usage by giving circulation only to a pure currency.

"To this representation the rulers of Bhoat replied that the amount of base Mehnder-mulli then in their country was very considerable; that the suppression of it would consequently be attended with great loss to their people; and that, therefore, they could not agree to the introduction of the pure Mehnder-mulli proposed by the Maharajah, but must desire that the Goorkhas would continue to supply them with the adulterated coin.

"Nine or ten years elapsed in this negociation between the two governments without their being able to fix on any plan of accommodation. At length the Goorkha envoy proposed that, as they could not stop the circulation of the base coin with which they had been supplied, they should, at least, establish a just rate of exchange between the base and pure coinage, to the end that the merchants of either country might stand in their commercial transactions on the same footing as formerly. The Bhootias, however, would by no means consent to such a regulation; but, on the contrary, absolutely directed that the base and genuine money should be considered, in all negociations of trade, as one and the same; the consequence of which was that for three or four years there was no sort of traffic carried on between the two countries. The circulation of the Nepaulian coin accordingly ceased (i.e. in Tibet). The Goorkha, nevertheless, continuing to retain his friendly disposition towards the Bhootias, endeavoured to prevail on them to depute some respectable person to the common boundary, there to meet and, in concert with deputies from Nepaul, devise some arrangement for the mutual benefit of the two states, as, without a speedy adjustment of the matter, it was evident that the trade of the two countries must be inevitably ruined. The Bhootias, however, were so far from listening to this reasonable proposal, that they, on the contrary, sent word vauntingly to the Goorkha that they had constructed a new road through the plain or valley of Tingri; that they were establishing a post on the common frontier; and that they had assembled an army of 125,000 men, and that, if the Goorkha wished for war, he was welcome to advance."[1]

The profits made by the Nepal Government on the silver coinage for Tibet are said by Kirkpatrick to have been a lakh of rupees annually.[2] He adds: "It is to be observed that all silver brought into Nepaul from Tibet, in the way of commerce, must be carried to the mint at Khatmanda, no silver bullion being allowed to pass into Hindostan. In exchange for his bullion the merchant receives Nepaul rupees, the Government deriving a profit of twelve per cent. from the transaction, four per cent. being charged on account of coinage and eight arising from the alloy of the rupee.

"With respect to gold, it has usually been a monopoly in the hands of Government, who obliged the traders from Tibet to sell it at the mint at the rate of eight rupees per tolah, whence the Ticksâli[3] retails it sometimes at the advanced price of fourteen rupees per tolah."[4]

So, altogether, the Newār Government made a large profit out of their monopoly of the coinage for Tibet.

Since the Goorkha conquest, Nepal has not again coined for

[1] Op. cit., pp. 339–40.
[2] Op. cit., p. 211.
[3] A Nepalese official.
[4] Op. cit., pp. 211–12.

Tibet, though, since the conclusion of the war, the Nepalese-Gorkha mohars have passed freely current in Tibet along with the Tibetan currency and are called *chö-tang* or '*tang-kas* for cutting,' owing to those being the *tang-ka* that is generally subdivided.

The coin of Jaya Raṇajita (Pl. II, Fig. 5) is known in Tibet as the *nag tang*, or 'black tang-ka.' There are a large number of these coins still in circulation, and many years of grease have made them black enough to deserve their name. A large number of these coins are also still current in Bhutan.

That the mohars of this first type were the design coined primarily for the Tibet coinage, and were consequently continued for that purpose, is supported by the fact that we find other coins of an entirely different device and character struck by the same kings, and even in the same year, reserved, no doubt, for the currency within Nepal. An example of this are the coins of Jaya Raṇajita Malla of Bhātgāon (Nos. 5 and 6; Pl. II, Figs. 4 and 8); of Pratāpa Malla of Kāṭhmāṇḍū (Nos. 11 and 12; Pl. II, Figs. 10 and 12); and Śrīnivāsa Malla of Pātan (Nos. 53 and 54; Pl. V, Figs. 3 and 4).

Besides the silver coinage there was until recently a copper currency of rough unstamped lumps of copper, called *ḍhebuā*, corresponding to the 'dumpy pice' that were formerly current in India. Four of these *ḍhebuās* make a *gaṇḍa*, and 25 *gaṇḍas* are equal to one rupee; so that 12½ *gaṇḍas* or 50 *ḍhebuās* were equal to the mohar. With the exception of Jaya Prakāśa Malla, none of the Newār kings coined silver coins of less denomination than the half mohar (called *sukā*, *sukī*, or *sikī*) and the quarter mohar (called *do-ānī*), and as 6¼ *gaṇḍas* or 25 *ḍhebuās* were equal to the *sukā*, and 3 *gaṇḍas* or 12 *ḍhebuās* equal to the *do-ānī*, the copper currency was in accordance with the silver coinage. As regards Jaya Prakāśa Malla's coins of smaller value, they probably were never in general circulation.

The Gorkhās, however, who adopted the Newār system of silver coinage, carried out its subdivisions to lower denominations, and there are thus under the Gorkhās two systems of currency below the mohar—the old Newār system of 'Pacis Gaṇḍa,' to which the Gorkhās subsequently added a coin called *dyāk*, equivalent to the Indian double pice; and the silver system of 'Sohra Gaṇḍa.' The two systems are given below.

The Pacīs Gaṇḍa System.

1 mohar	= 2 sukā, sukī, or sikī.
1 sukā, etc.	= 2 do-ānī = 6½ gaṇḍas of copper ḍhebuās or 25 ḍhebuās.
1 do-ānī	= 3 gaṇḍas of copper ḍhebuās or 12 ḍhebuas.
1 do-ānī	= 6 dyāks (double pice), a Gorkhā coin.
1 dyāk	= 2 ḍhebuās (*Newār*), or 2 paisā (Gorkhā).
1 ḍhebuā	= 4 (copper) dāms.
1 (copper) dām or paisā dām	= 2 phokā dāms, or chūn dāms.

The Sohra Gaṇḍa System.

1 mohar	= 2 sukā, sukī, or sikī.
1 sukā, etc. (½ mohar)	= 2 do-ānī.
1 do-ānī (¼ mohar)	= 2 ek-ānī.
1 ek-ānī (⅛ mohar)	= 2 ādhā-ānī.
1 ādhā-ānī (1/16 mohar)	= 1 paisā mohar (silver pice).
1 paisā mohar (1/32 mohar)	= 2 do-dām (the silver leaf), also called ādhā-paisā.

The value of the silver anna is nominally six copper pice, but the exchange value in practice seems to vary at certain places, as I have heard from Nepalis that it is equal to seven copper pice.

In the lists of Newār and of Gorkhā coins I have called the *sukā*, *do-ānī*, *ek-ānī*, etc., by their fractional part of the mohar.

To follow the coinage of the Malla dynasties it is necessary to give a brief sketch of the history of the three kingdoms of Bhātgāon, Kāṭhmāṇḍū (also known as

Kāntipur), and Pātan (also known as Lalitapur). In Table I, I have given contemporary lists of the kings of each of the three kingdoms. The names of the first seven kings of Bhātgāon and also the first eight kings of Kāṭhmāṇḍū, whose coins are not known, are taken from the Vaṁśāvalī, and correspond with those given by Professor Bendall in Table II of his "Journey in Nepal"[1] and Table II of his "History of Nepal and surrounding Kingdoms."[2]

The subsequent names for the three kingdoms are fixed by their coins, in addition to the Vaṁśāvalī. Those for Bhātgāon, viz., Jagatprakāśa, Jitamitra, Bhūpatīndra, and Raṇajita Mallas, are as given in Professor Bendall's tables, but I have made certain additions to the kings of Kāṭhmāṇḍū and Pātan which do not appear in those tables, and which I therefore give below.

Kāṭhmāṇḍū.

1. I have added the names of the thirteenth king Jaya Mahīpendra and the fourteenth Jaya Pārthivendra, which do not occur in Professor Bendall's tables. The Vaṁśāvalī states that Pratāpa Malla had four sons—Pārthivendra Malla, Nṛpendra Malla (also called Mahīpatīndra Malla), and Chakravartīndra Malla. By the advice of a Swāmī he "left his throne for a time to be filled in turn by his four sons . . . Chakravartendra reigned only for one day, but the other three sons reigned for their three years."

The reigns of Chakravartīndra and Nṛpendra are known, that of Pārthivendra is now shown by his coins (Pl. III, Figs. 2 and 3), and, as the statement of the Vaṁśāvalī is thus correct as regards the other three

[1] "A Journey of Literary and Archæological Research in Northern India," by Cecil Bendall, Cambridge, 1886.

[2] "History of Nepal and surrounding Kingdoms," by Cecil Bendall: J.A.S.B., vol. lxxii, pt. 1, p. 1.

sons, it may also be taken to be correct as regards the remaining one, Mahīpendra Malla.

2. Professor Bendall shows Jyoti Prakāśa Malla, the twentieth king, in brackets, as not having reigned; and, referring to a coin bearing his name of date 1749 A.D., notes: "[coin struck apparently in a rebellion—see Wright, p. 224]." Jyoti Prakāśa's coin (No. 49; Pl. IV, Fig. 15), however, bears date 866 N.S., corresponding to 1746 A.D., which shows that coins were struck in his name both in 1746 and in 1749 A.D. Jyoti Prakāśa was the infant son of Jaya Prakāśa, aged 2½ years, whom the nobles, being discontented with Jaya Prakāśa, set up as king under the regency of his mother, Queen Dayāvatī, and drove Jaya Prakāśa from the kingdom. The Vaṁśāvalī says that he spent two and a half years in exile, when he received a miraculous sword from a devotee at Gujhesvarī, which enabled him to return and regain his kingdom.[1] It is thus clear that Jyoti Prakāśa reigned under the regency of his mother for that period.

The Vaṁśāvalī gives the name of his regent mother as Dayāvatī. I do not, however, find any coin bearing this queen's name, as would be expected if she had been regent. But there is a coin of Jananī, Jaya Lakṣmī Devī (No. 50; Pl. VI, Fig. 12), which bears date of the same year, which would seem to be the title of the queen regent.

Pātan.

3. Siddhi Narasiṁha is shown by Professor Bendall as the first king of the separate kingdom of Pātan. I have, however, shown the division as dating from Hariharasiṁha, as the Vaṁśāvalī states that he "went to rule over Pātan in the lifetime of his father Śivasiṁha," and although, on succeeding his father subsequently, he ruled over the two kingdoms, Pātan as a separate kingdom had already been constituted, and was regarded as such. This is also shown

[1] Wright, p. 224.

by the fact that, although on his father's death Harihara simha succeeded in ousting his elder brother Lakṣmī Narasimha from the kingdom of Kāthmāṇḍū, it was Lakṣmī Narasimha who succeeded to that kingdom as the son of Śivasimha, while Hariharasimha's son, Siddhi Narasimha, succeeded his father as ruler of the separate kingdom of Pātan.

4. I have added the name of Jaya Indra Malla, the fifth king. His name does not occur in the Vaṁśāvalī or in Professor Bendall's table, but the date on his coin (No. 61; Pl. V, Fig. 11) is 826 N.S., corresponding with 1706 A.D., which places him as the successor of Jaya Yoga Narendra.

5. The name of Jaya Loka Prakāśa does not occur from his coin, but is given in Bendall's table. The date on his coin (No. 62; not illustrated) is 827 N.S., corresponding to 1707 A.D., on which his name occurs together with that of Yogamatī Devī. He was no doubt a minor son of Yoga Narendra, and reigned under the regency of his mother Yogamatī; for there is an inscription which records that Yogamatī Devī dedicated a temple in memory of her deceased son Loka Prakāśa.[1]

6. I have added the name of Vīra Narasimha, the seventh ruler. His name does not occur in the Vaṁśāvalī or in Wright's table. His coin (No. 63; Pl. V, Fig. 12) bears date 829 N.S., corresponding with 1709 A.D., and as his name also occurs jointly with that of Yogamatī Devī, he was also, no doubt, another minor son of Yoga Narendra, who succeeded on Loka Prakāśa's death, and for whom his mother ruled as regent.

7. I have shown the name of Jaya Vīra Mahīndra or Mahīndra Siṁha Deva of Kāṭhmāṇḍū as the eighth ruler, as the Vaṁśāvalī states that he also ruled over Pātan, and he is consequently shown as the fifth ruler

[1] Inscription No. 22. *Indian Antiquary*, vol. ix, p. 192.

in Bendall's table. The statement of the Vaṁśāvalī as to Vīra Mahīndra's reign over Pātan, however, appears to be very doubtful. The Vaṁśāvalī says: "After him (viz. Yoganarendra) Mahīpatīndra or Mahīndra Siṁha Malla (Rāja of Kāntipur) became also Rāja of Pātan . . . On the 11th of Bhador Badi N.S. 842 (A.D. 1722) Mahīndra Malla died. Jaya Yoga Prakāśa succeeded him."[1] From the coins of the preceding three rulers, however, it is quite clear that Vīra Mahīndra did not, as stated, succeed Yoga Narendra, and from the coins of Hṛdi Narasiṁha, 1715 A.D., it is also quite certain that he did not reign till 1722 A.D. and that he was not succeeded by Jaya Yoga Prakāśa. The statement of the Vaṁśāvalī is, therefore, incorrect on every point, and so it is very doubtful whether Vīra Mahīndra ever reigned over Pātan at all. If he did, it was between Vīra Narasiṁha and Hṛdi Narasiṁha.

8. I have shown the name of Hṛdi Narasiṁha as the ninth ruler. His name does not occur in the Vaṁśāvalī or in Bendall's table. His date, from his coins (Nos. 64 and 65; Pl. VI, Figs. 1 and 2), is 835 N.S., corresponding to 1715 A.D.

9. I have shown Raṇajita Malla of Bhātgāon as the thirteenth ruler. His name is not shown in Bendall's table. The Vaṁśāvalī says that Rājya Prakāśa Malla "was a pacific man and worshipped a number of Saligrams. The six Pradhāns, taking advantage of his simplicity, deprived him of his eyesight. He did not long survive this, and after his death the Pradhān of the Dhālāchekācha caste brought the Raja of Bhātgāon, Raṇajita Malla, and made him Raja of Pātan also. After a year's reign, however, the Pradhāns drove him away, when he had gone to bathe at Sankhamula."[2]

10. I have shown Jaya Prakāśa of Kāṭhmāṇḍū as the fourteenth ruler. The Vaṁśāvalī says that after the

[1] Wright, p. 248.
[2] Wright, p. 250.

expulsion of Raṇajita "the Pradhāns made Jaya Prakāśa, the Raja of Kāntipur, Raja of Pātan also, and he ruled over both cities . . . Jaya Prakāśa ruled for one or two years; but the Pradhāns were afraid of him, and one day, when he went to Tekhu-dobhān to bathe, they expelled him. They then installed as Raja a grandson (daughter's son) of Visṇu Malla, named Viśvajita Malla, who reigned for four years. The six Pradhāns were soon displeased with him, and, in order to get rid of him, they accused him of adultery with one of their wives, and killed him at the door of Taleju."[1]

Almost all the Malla coins, except those of the Tibet coinage, bear the sword (*khaḍga*), the emblem of sovereignty, which is generally combined with a garland. The other non-religious symbols are the mace and the lion. The remaining symbols are all religious. Of these, the one most generally found on the coins is the trident of Siva, and the others are the Aṣṭa Maṅgala[2] (the eight Buddhist signs of good luck); the shell, *śāṅkha*; the holy water vase, *kalaśa* or *kumbha*; the vase for offerings, with cover in form of a *stūpa*; the discus, *cakra*; and the double-drum, *ḍamaru*, of form like an hour-glass, used in tantric worship.

With the exception of the trident, these symbols are all of them common to both the Hindu and Buddhist religions, though the interpretation given to them differs according to the religion.

The trident (*triśula*) appears on the reverse of the coins of the earliest type, in the small central circle, which, as already noted, was imitated from that in the coin of the

[1] Wright, pp. 250, 251.

[2] The *Aṣṭa Maṅgala* are (1) *Matsya*, the two golden fish; (2) *Catra*, the umbrella of sovereignty; (3) *Śāṅkha*, the hollowed conch shell for blowing as a trumpet; (4) *Śrīvatsa*, a lucky diagram, also known as "Buddha's entrails"; (5) *Dvaja*, the banner of victory; (6) *Kalaśa*, vase of holy water; (7) *Padma*, the lotus; and (8) *Cakra*, the wheel of the law.

Bengal king Ghiyāṣ-ud-dīn Maḥmūd. On these coins it always bears the same form, with two streamers attached to the shaft. All the mohars of Bhātgāon are of this pattern, except the mohar of Raṇajita Malla (Pl. I, Fig. 6), which he copied from that of Cakravartīndra Malla of Kāthmāṇḍū. On the mohars of Kāṭhmāṇḍū, subsequent to those of the early type, the trident appears with plain shaft without streamers, though on one of the smaller coins, a quarter mohar of Rūpamatī Devī, the consort of Pratāpa Malla (Pl. II, Fig. 11), it follows the earlier form, and has small streamers. In two coins of Jaya Prakāśa Malla (Nos. 37 and 38 ; Pl. IV, Figs. 7 and 8) the trident has flowers springing from its shaft. In the kingdom of Pātan Buddhism was much stronger than at Bhātgāon and Kāṭhmāṇḍū, and consequently the Sivaite emblem of the trident does not appear on the coins of the early type, its place being taken in the coins of Siddhi Narasiṁha by the lion which forms the rebus of his name (Pl. V, Figs. 1 and 2), and in the coin of Śrīnivāsa by the legend which is continued on the reverse of the coin (Pl. V, Fig. 3). For the same reason the Sivaite emblem of the double-drum (*ḍamaru*), which occurs on these coins of Bhātgāon and Kāṭhmāṇḍū, is omitted from the Pātan coins, its place being taken by the Buddhist emblem of the lotus flower. The trident does not also appear on the earlier coins of Yoga Narendra Malla. It first appears on his coin of 1700 A.D., a coin of an entirely different character to his previous ones, which bore only Buddhist symbols, and it then appears on the coins of all the subsequent kings, except those of Hṛdi Narasiṁha Malla.

The double-drum (*ḍamaru*), which is also a Sivaite emblem, and which occurs on the coins of the early type of Bhātgāon and Kāṭhmāṇḍū as already mentioned, does not appear on those of Pātan.

The Aṣṭa Maṅgala, the eight Buddhist signs of good luck, do not appear on the coins of Bhātgāon which adhered to the early type. In Kāṭhmāṇḍū they first appear on the coin of Bhūpālendra Malla (No. 20; Pl. III, Fig. 4), and, after that, are the standard device for the obverse of the mohar of every succeeding king (Pl. III, Figs. 5–12, and Pl. IV, Figs. 2–6 and 15), with the exception of one coin of Jaya Jagajjaya Malla (No. 31; Pl. IV, Fig. 1). They do not occur on any of the coins of Pātan, and although Yoga Prakāśa Malla copied the device of the circle surrounded by eight petals (No. 66; Pl. VI, Fig. 3), the petals contain the legend, as on the reverse of the Kāṭhmāṇḍū coins.

The vase of holy water (*kalaśa*) appears on the quarter mohar of Bhūpatīndra Malla (Pl. II, Fig. 5), and on the half and quarter mohars of Raṇajita Malla of Bhātgāon (Pl. II, Figs. 6 and 7). Also on the mohar of Pārthivendra Malla of Kāṭhmāṇḍū (No. 17; Pl. III, Fig. 2), and of Śrīnivāsa Malla of Pātan (No. 54; Pl. V, Fig. 4).

The vase of offerings, with cover in the form of a stūpa, appears on the quarter mohars of Jaya Mahīndra Malla (No. 27; Pl. III, Fig. 10) and Jaya Jagajjaya Malla (No. 30; Pl. III, Fig. 13) of Kāṭhmāṇḍū, and on the mohars of Yoga Narendra Malla (Nos. 55–58; Pl. V, Figs. 5–8); of Jaya Indra Malla (No. 61; Pl. V, Fig. 11); Vīra Narasiṁha Malla (No. 63; Pl. V, Fig. 12); and the quarter mohar of Jananī Lakṣmī Devī (No. 50; Pl. VI, Fig. 12) of Pātan.

The shell (*śaṅkha*) is a symbol peculiar to the coins of Kāṭhmāṇḍū. It only appears on one coin of Pātan, a mohar of Yoga Narendra Malla (No. 57; Pl. V, Fig. 7), and on one coin of Bhātgāon, the mohar of Raṇajita Malla (No. 6; Pl. II, Fig. 8), which is copied exactly from the mohar of Cakravartīndra Malla of Kāṭhmāṇḍū (Pl. II, Fig. 13). M. Terrien de La Couperie, writing on the silver coinage of Tibet, says that the coins of the three Nepal kingdoms "were generally distinguished by a shell for Bhātgāon, a trisul (trident) for Pātan, and a sword for Kāṭhmāṇḍū."[1] This, however, is quite incorrect. The shell does not occur at all on the coins of Bhātgāon with the one special exception noted; the trident is conspicuous by its absence from the early type of coins of Pātan, and did not appear on the subsequent coins until much later than at Kāṭhmāṇḍū; and the sword, which was the Newār emblem of sovereignty, is common to all the three kingdoms, and, in fact, the earliest coins on which it appears are those of Pātan (Pl. V, Figs. 1, 2, and 3).

The discus of Viṣṇu (*cakra*) appears on the coin of Cakravartīndra Malla of Kāṭhmāṇḍū (No. 15; Pl. II, Fig. 13), and may have been adopted partly as a rebus for his name. It appears together with the shell, an association which may be due to the fact that the *cakra* and the shell each supported on a pillar appear as symbols in front of the temple of Cangu Nārāyaṇa.[2] It similarly appears on the coin of Raṇajita Malla of Bhātgāon, which, as already mentioned, he copied from Cakravartīndra's coin. The *cakra* also appears on a pedestal in a form similar to that which it bears surmounting the pillar in front of the temple of Cangu Nārāyaṇa, of which it is probably a representation on the quarter mohar of Jananī Kumudinī Devī of Kāthmāṇḍū (No. 39; Pl. IV, Fig. 9), and the mohars of Jaya Indra Malla and Vīra Narasiṁha Malla (Nos. 61 and 63; Pl. V, Figs. 11 and 12).

The mace (*gada*) appears on the coin of Cakravartīndra, and on its copy of Raṇajita Malla, and also on the half mohar of Raṇajita Malla (No. 7; Pl. II, Fig. 7), where its head has been developed into a flower in a very artistic manner. It also appears, in combination with the shell, on coins of Yoga Narendra Malla of Pātan (Nos. 56, 57, and 58; Pl. V, Figs. 6, 7, and 8).

[1] Terrien de La Couperie, "Silver Coinage of Tibet": Numismatic Chronicle, 3rd series, vol. i, p. 340.

[2] Professor Lévi gives an illustration of this temple: "Le Népal," vol. i, p. 231.

The equilateral triangle, known as *vāṇāstra*, which is a conventional representation of a drawn bow, appears on the reverse of the coin of Cakravartīndra and its copy of Raṇajita Malla (Nos. 15 and 6; Pl. II, Figs. 13 and 8), and on Raṇajita Malla's half mohar (Pl. II, Fig. 7), and on the reverse of the mohars of Jaya Prakāśa Malla (Nos. 35 and 36; Pl. IV, Figs. 5 and 6). Equilateral triangles also appear on the coins of Śrīnivāsa, Yoga Narendra, and Vīra Narasiṁha of Pātan (Nos. 54, 56, and 63; Pl. V, Figs. 4, 6, and 12), but in this case they appear to be merely to form geometrical designs. The triangle (*trikoṇa*) is also the special symbol of the Newār goddess Gujheswarī, which may account for its use on these coins.

The *Svastika*, Fly-foot Cross, appears only on the coins of Yoga Narendra Malla of Pātan (Nos. 55, 56, and 57; Pl. V, Figs. 5, 6, and 7). This design of the double *svastika* no doubt suggested to the Gorkhā conqueror Pṛthvī Nārāyaṇa Sāha the design for his mohar, which has remained the standard design of the Gorkhā coinage (Pl. VII, Fig. 1), and which was copied by his brother Dala Mardana Sāha when king of Pātan (No. 75; Pl. VI, Fig. 13).

The remaining symbol found on the Newār coins is the lion, which appears as a rebus for the name 'Siṁha' on the coins of Siddhi Narasiṁha (Nos. 51, 52; Pl. V, Figs. 1, 2) and Hṛdi Narasiṁha of Pātan (Nos. 64, 65; Pl. VI, Figs. 1, 2). It is of the same design, facing left with the tail curled over its back, as the lion on the coins of Mānāṅka and Aṁśu-varman, from which it is no doubt copied.

Besides the use of religious symbols, the kings of Pātan inscribed the names of the national deities on their coins. Only two of the kings of Kāṭhmāṇḍū, Jaya Vīra Mahīndra Malla and Jaya Prakāśa Malla, followed this practice, and no names of deities appear on the coins of Bhātgāon which adhered to the early type. The names of the following deities occur on the coins of Pātan and of Jaya Vīra Mahīndra Malla, and Jaya Prakāśa Malla of Kāṭhmāṇḍū.

The name of Lokanātha appears on the coins of Yoga Narendra Malla (Nos. 55, 56, 57, 58, and, together with the name of the goddess Taleju Māju on coin No. 60); of Jaya Indra Malla (No. 61); of Vīra Narasiṁha Malla (No. 63); of Jaya Viṣṇu Malla (No. 67); of Rājya Prakāśa Malla (Nos. 69, 70, 71, 72); and of Viśvajita Malla (Nos. 73 and 74) of Pātan. It also appears on the coin of Jaya Vīra Mahīndra Malla of Kāṭhmāṇḍū (No. 24).

The name of the goddess Kaluṇāmaya, or Karuṇāmaya, appears on the coins of Queen Yogamatī and Loka Prakāśa Malla (No. 62); of Hṛdi Narasiṁha Malla (Nos. 64, 65); of Yoga Prakāśa Malla (No. 66); of Jaya Viṣṇu Malla (No. 68); and of Dala Mardana Sāha (No. 75) of Pātan, and on a coin of Jaya Vīra Mahīndra of Kāthmāndū (No. 25).

The name of the goddess Taleju Māju appears, together with that of Lokanātha, on a coin of Yoga Narendra Malla of Pātan (No. 60), and together with that of the goddess Kumārī Māju on a coin of Jaya Prakāśa Malla of Kāṭhmāṇḍū (No. 36).

The name of the goddess Gujheswarī appears on a quarter mohar of Jaya Prakāśa Malla of Kāṭhmāṇḍū (No. 45), and, together with that of Paśupati, on another quarter mohar of this king (No. 40). The latter coin is peculiar, as it only bears the name of these two deities without the name of the king or queen, and is the only example of this in the Newār coinage, although it occurred in the ancient coins of Paśupati.

A feature of the Newār coinage is the inclusion of the names of the queen consorts on the coins. Besides the names of the queens who were regents for their minor sons, as Jananī Jaya Lakṣmī Devī (No. 50), regent for her son Jyoti Prakāśa Malla, and Yogamatī Devī (No. 62), regent for her son Loka Prakāśa Malla, and again (No. 63) for her son Vīra Narasiṁha Malla, the names of the consorts of the reigning kings frequently appear on the coins. In the Kāṭhmāṇḍū coins the queens' names only appear on the quarter mohar (*do-ānī*). These are Rūpamati Devī, queen of Pratāpa Malla (No. 14): Rājya Lakṣmī Devī, queen of Pārthivendra Malla (No. 19): Mahīndra Lakṣmī Devī, queen of Jaya Vīra Mahīndra (No. 27); and Kumudinī Devī, queen of Jaya Jagajjaya Malla (No. 30). In the Pāṭan coins the queens' names occur on the mohars, as follows: Yoga Lakṣmī Devī and Narendra Lakṣmī Devī, together on the coin of Yoga Narendra Malla (No. 55); Narendra Lakṣmī Devī and Pratāpa Lakṣmī Devī, together on another of the coins of the same king (No. 56); also Yoga Lakṣmī Devī, singly on another coin (No. 57); and Bhāgavatī Devī appears on the coin of Jaya Indra Malla (No. 61).

A characteristic of the coins of the Kāṭhmāṇḍū dynasty is the use of flowers as a decoration on the coins of several of the rulers. The first coin decorated with flowers is the mohar of Pratāpa Malla (No. 12) and his square double mohar (No. 13), the mohars of Cakravartīndra Malla (No. 15), Jaya Nṛpendra Malla (No. 16), and Pārthivendra Malla (No. 18). After that the mohars assumed a more or less fixed type, but in these the device was itself based on a flower, being the petals of the lotus flower on the obverse and its leaves on the reverse. The Nepalese as a race are very fond of flowers, and even the poorest use them as personal adornment.

The Malla kings did not generally inscribe titles on their coins, but only their names. The following kings, however, inscribed titles on their coins: Jaya Śrīnivāsa Malla of Pāṭan took the title "Nepāleśvara" (No. 54), which was also assumed by Jaya Bhūpālendra Malla (No. 20), and also by Jaya Jagajjaya Malla (No. 28) of Kāṭhmāṇḍū, as "Nepāleśvara Rājendra."

Bhūpālendra Malla also assumed the title of "Girīndra Rāja Rājendra," Lord over the kings of the Hills (No. 21), and the title was also assumed as "Nepāleśvara Girīndra" by Jaya Bhāskara (No. 22) and Jaya Vīra Mahīndra (No. 26). The title of "Kavīndra," King of Poets, as already noticed, was assumed by Pratāpa Malla (No. 12) and by Bhūpālendra Malla (No. 21). The title of "Nepāla Chuḍāmaṇi," Jewel on the Crown of Nepal, was assumed by Yoga Narendra Malla of Pātan (No. 58) and "Nepāleśvara Chuḍāmaṇi" (No. 59), and Bhūpālendra Malla of Kāṭhmāṇḍū subsequently uses the title as "Chuḍāmaṇi Samrāṭ" (No. 21), the Jewel on the Crown of the Empire.

Yoga Narendra Malla of Pātan uses the title of "Saṁgītārṇṇava - Pāraga," skilled in music (No. 55), referring to his proficiency in that art.

The general characteristics of the Malla coinage have now been considered, but there are one or two coins which call for individual notice.

The design of the mohar of Cakravartīndra, 1669 A.D. (No. 15; Pl. II, Fig. 13), has been already alluded to. The device of this coin is supposed by the Newārs to have been particularly unlucky, and to have caused Cakravartīndra's death. The Vaṁśāvalī says: "The inscription on Cakravartīndra's coin, devised by the Svāmī, consists of a triangular Bāṇāstra (bow and arrow), Pās (noose), Aṅkus (the iron hook for driving an elephant), Kamal (a lotus), Chāmar (a yak's tail), and Saṁbat 789. This device caused his death." To this Dr. Wright adds a footnote that "a bow and arrow are ominous of death, but nevertheless the water in which such a coin is dipped possesses the quality of causing a speedy delivery in child-bed. These coins, which are very rare, are still used for this purpose."[1] This is, as Dr. Wright remarks, the general belief with regard to this coin, and I was told of

[1] Wright's History, p. 220.

this virtue when I obtained my specimen of the coin. It is curious that, with such a belief as to the unluckiness of this coin, Raṇajita Malla should have copied the device.

Jaya Pratâpa Malla imitated the Persian inscription on the coins of the Moghul Emperors with a floral decoration of the field. His coin which bears this device is dated 775 N.S. or 1755 A.D. (No. 12; Pl. II, Fig. 12).

The upper line of characters on the reverse appears to be intended for the commencement and last portion of "Shâh 'Alamgīr," from whose coins Pratâpa Malla would therefore appear to have copied them. This introduction of Persian characters, which the minters failed to correctly imitate, is characteristic of Pratâpa Malla, who prided himself on his extensive knowledge, and composed a prayer to Svayambhû, in which he introduced Persian and various other characters, and had inscribed on a stone at that temple. It was after composing this prayer that Pratâpa Malla assumed the title of "Kavīndra," King of Poets, which appears on this coin. Pratâpa Malla's device of this coin was copied by Jaya Nṛpendra and Jaya Pârthivendra (Pl. III, Figs. 1 and 3), and two lines of meaningless imitation Persian characters appear on the reverse of mohars of Jaya Bhâskara, Vīra Mahīndra, Jaya Jagajjaya Mallas of Kâṭhmâṇḍû, and were also adopted by Jaya Viṣṇu and Râjya Prakâśa Mallas of Pâtan on the obverse of their coins (Nos. 67 and 69).

Jaya Bhûpâlendra (1682 A.D.) also assumed the title of Kavīndra (No. 21). He originated the device of eight lotus petals surrounding a central circle, with the *aṣṭa-maṅgala* within the petals for the obverse, and a similar arrangement of eight leaves for the reverse, which remained the standard device for the coins of the subsequent rulers.

His design, as modified by his successor Jaya Bhâskara Malla (No. 22; Pl. III, Fig. 5), was copied by the Government of Tibet for their coinage when Tibet gave up obtaining their coinage from Nepal, and with the substitution of a floral design the central circle on the obverse, and a wheel within the central circle on the reverse, is the "*Gah-dan tanka*," which has continued to be the standard coinage of Tibet up to the present time.

The latest mohars of Jaya Viṣṇu Malla of Pātan (No. 67), and all those of his successor Rājya Prakāśa Malla (Nos. 69 to 72), bear on the reverse the name of Vīra Yoga Narendra Malla. The reason of this would appear to be because Yoga Narendra Malla, who from grief at the death of his son and heir relinquished the kingdom and went away as an ascetic, was supposed to be still living, and the government of the country to be carried on by his successors on his behalf. The Vaṁśāvalī says: "He told the minister that as long as the face of his statue remained bright and untarnished, and the bird on its head had not flown away, he would know that the Rājā was alive, and should cherish and respect his memory. For this reason a mattress is still every night laid in a room in the front of the Darbar, and the window is left open."[1] To this Dr. Wright adds a footnote that this is still done, as the face of the statue remains bright.

Rājya Prakāśa Malla,[2] Jaya Viṣṇu Malla's successor, also, for the same reason, inscribed the name of Vīra Yoga Narendra Malla on all his coins (Nos. 69 to 72). In coins Nos. 69, 70, and 71 the reverse is the same as Jaya Viṣṇu's coin No. 67, but in coin No. 72 the device is different, which shows that the insertion of Yoga Narendra Malla's name was not merely due to a continuance of the reverse of Jaya Viṣṇu's coin.

[1] Wright, p. 248.

[2] Rājya Prakāśa Malla was the younger brother of Jaya Prakāśa Malla of Kāṭhmāṇḍū, by whom he was expelled from the country, as the sepoys wanted to make him king instead of Jaya Prakāśa. As Jaya Viṣṇu Malla had no son he appointed Rājya Prakāśa as his successor, which was accepted by the people (Wright, p. 249).

THE GORKHĀ COINAGE.

The following is a brief sketch of the history of the Gorkhā dynasty. All references to Gorkhā coins which follow are to the serial number in the list of Gorkhā coins, which form a separate series to those of the Newār coins which have been already considered.

The Gorkhās claim to be descended from the Rajputs of Chitor, whose dynasty commences from Rṣirājā Bhaṭṭāraka, about the year 80 A.D. According to their history, after the taking of Chitor by Ala-uddin in 1289 A.D., one part of the survivors went and settled at Udaipur, and another, under Manmatha Rana, settled at Ujjain. Manmatha Raṇa's younger son Mica Khān,[1] however, with his followers, migrated to the Himalayas and settled at Noakoṭ,[2] where they made themselves masters of the neighbouring territories.

In 1559 A.D. they again divided. Dravya Sāha, a younger son, obtained the sovereignty of the town and territory of Gorkhā, forty miles west of Kāṭhmāṇḍū, from which the Gorkhās have taken their name. Intent on pushing their conquests eastward, Dambara Sāha (1633–1642 A.D.) invaded the territories of Pratāpa Malla, but was repulsed. Nara Bhūpāla Sāha (1716–1742 A.D.), the father of Pṛthvī Nārāyaṇa, taking advantage of the internal dissensions between the Nepalese kingdoms, again invaded Nepal, but was stopped by the Ṭhākurs of Noakoṭ[3] and forced to retreat.

On his father's death, Pṛthvī Nārāyaṇa came to the throne at the age of 12, and at once proceeded to

[1] He is the 36th Raja in the Genealogy (Wright's "History of Nepal," p. 276).

[2] Not the Noakot near Kāṭhmāṇḍū, but another far to the west.

[3] Viz. Noakot in Nepal (Wright, 197).

attack Noakot,[1] which belonged to the kingdom of Kāṭhmāṇḍū. He was, however, repulsed by Jaya Prakāśa and forced to retire, but succeeded in his second attack eight years later (1750 or 1751).[2] At this time he also went to reside with Raṇajita Malla at Bhātgāon, where he became a close friend of Raṇajita's son and heir Vīra Narasiṁha Malla, and where he continued to reside for several years. He there stirred up the seven illegitimate sons of Raṇajita Malla, with the promise that he would obtain the kingdom for them, to conspire against Vīra Narasiṁha, whom they eventually contrived to poison; the Vaṁśāvalī, euphemistically, records that "he died suddenly." Raṇajita Malla called in Pṛthvī Nārāyaṇa to assist him in his quarrel with Jaya Prakāśa, of Kāṭhmāṇḍū. Pṛthvī Nārāyaṇa seized the opportunity to attack Kīrtipur, a town on an eminence about three miles south-west of Kāṭhmāṇḍū, which was subject to the kingdom of Pātan, and which, from its position, was considered impregnable. The king of Pātan did not attempt to defend it, but Jaya Prakāśa went to its assistance and defeated Pṛthvī Nārāyaṇa, who was forced to retire. The people of Kīrtipur then asked Jaya Prakāśa to become their king, and the nobles (Thāris) assembled to make the town over to him. He, however, insulted them and had one of their number imprisoned, in revenge for which they handed over several places in the kingdom of Kāṭhmāṇḍū to Pṛthvī Nārāyaṇa, who also again laid siege for several months to Kīrtipur, but was obliged eventually to give it up. He then attacked the king of Lamji, a neighbouring state, and after several battles concluded an agreement with him and returned towards Kīrtipur.[3] The three Nepalese kingdoms then attempted to combine against their common danger and

[1] Noakot in Nepal.
[2] Lévi, "Le Népal," vol. ii, p. 271.
[3] Wright, pp. 224, 225.

attacked Pṛthvī Nārāyaṇa, but after a protracted siege Kīrtipur was given up to Pṛthvī Nārāyaṇa by the noble whom Jaya Prakāśa had insulted and imprisoned. Pṛthvī Nārāyaṇa then invested Pātan, but the advance of the British troops under Captain Kinlock into the Terai (1767) caused him to withdraw. On Captain Kinlock's expedition having to retire on account of malaria and difficulty of communications, he laid siege to Kāṭhmāṇḍū, which he finally entered with scarcely any opposition on the 29th September, 1768, during the festival of the Indrajatra; when most of the inhabitants were feasting or drunk, Jaya Prakāśa sat in the temple of Taleju watching the fighting. At last, seeing that all was lost, he spread gunpowder on the steps of the temple and fled to Lalitapur, and taking the king Teja Narasiṁha with him, took refuge at Bhātgāon.[1] This gave Pṛthvī Nārāyaṇa both Kāṭhmāṇḍū and Pātan, and he then turned his attention to the town of Bhātgāon, which he succeeded in entering through the treachery of the illegitimate sons of Raṇajita Malla, whom he had won over, as already mentioned. Raṇajita was allowed to go to Benares, where he ended his days, Jaya Prakāśa was taken, at his own request, to Paśupati, where he died from the results of a wound he had received in the taking of Bhātgāon, and Teja Narasiṁha was imprisoned at Lakṣmīpur until his death, and thus the three Malla kingdoms came to an end in 1768 A.D.

Pṛthvī Nārāyaṇa was succeeded by his son Pratāpa Siṁha Sāha, who reigned for three years, 1775–8 A.D.[2] He was succeeded by his son Raṇa Bahādur Sāha, who was an infant, and whose mother, Rājendra Lakṣmī Devī, governed as Regent. From the death of Pratāpa Siṁha

[1] Wright, p. 232.

[2] The brief sketch of the history of the Gorkhā dynasty which follows is taken from Professor Lévi's "Népal," which is fuller and more complete than that given in Wright's History.

Sāha, the Gorkhā dynasty has been a succession of minor kings and regencies. The king has been merely a nominal ruler, the real government and power being in the hands of the Prime Minister. In 1795 Raṇa Bahādur Sāha, having attained majority, decided to reign himself, and arrested and imprisoned his uncle the minister. He had been married to Lalitā Tripurā Sundarī, a daughter of the Rāja of Gulmī, a neighbouring hill state. He, however, neglected her, and married a slave-girl, who appears from coin No. 35 to have assumed the title of Rāja Rājesvarī Devī. The name of Lalitā Tripurā Sundarī does not appear on the coins of this reign, though it appears on coins of his successor Rājendra Vikrama, together with that of Rājendra Lakṣmī. He also married Rājendra Lakṣmī Devī, the daughter of a Brahman, by whom he had a son, Girvāṇa Yuddha Vikrama Sāha. Being a Kṣatriya he could not marry a Brahman, and this and other acts of impiety so aroused the people against him that he was obliged to resign the throne, and his infant son Girvāṇa Yuddha Vikrama Sāha was appointed in 1800 A.D. with his mother Rājendra Lakṣmī Devī as Regent, and Damodar Pāṇḍe as Minister; as the senior queen Lalitā Tripurā Sundarī resolved to accompany her husband into exile. Rājendra Lakṣmī's name occurs on the coins both during the reign of her husband, as consort (No. 21) and as Regent for her son (No. 34).

In 1802 Tripurā Sundarī, tired of the ill-treatment of her husband, returned to Nepal, and was welcomed by the people, on which Raṇa Bahādur Sāha also returned, and assumed the government again in his son's name, until he was assassinated in 1807. Girvāṇa Yuddha died in 1816.

His minor son Rājendra Vikrama Sāha succeeded him under the regency of his grandmother Rājendra Lakṣmī Devī. Her name as Regent during this reign occurs, together with that of Tripurā Sundarī Devī, on coins

Nos. 64 and 65, and by itself as "Regent" on coin No. 69. In 1832 the old queen Tripurā Sundarī died.

Rājendra Vikrama had two wives, the first related to the Pāṇḍes and the second to the Thāpās, the two rival factions in the state, who devoted their influence to assisting their respective parties. In 1846 Rājendra Vikrama and his queen were expelled, and his minor son Surendra Vikrama Sāha was appointed as Regent with Jang Bahadur as his Minister. Rājendra Vikrama subsequently returned to Nepal and was imprisoned, where he died in 1847, and Surendra Vikrama then succeeded to the throne under a regency. In 1881 Surendra Vikrama died, after a purely nominal reign of 34 years, and was succeeded by his grandson, a child of six years, Pṛthvī Vīra Vikrama Sāha, who is the present King.

Pṛthvī Nārāyaṇa, on his conquest of the country, adopted the Newār system of coinage based on the standard of a silver mohar, and with the same fractional parts. The design of his mohar (No. 1; Pl. VII, Fig. 1), which has continued to be the standard design ever since, was also taken from the Newār coins, the design of the obverse, a square divided by a *svastika* having probably been suggested by the coins of Yoga Narendra Malla of Pātan (Pl. V; Figs. 5, 6, and 7) combined with the small central circle containing a trident with streamers on the current coins of Raṇajita Malla (Pl. II, Fig. 5) with which Pṛthvī Nārāyaṇa was familiar, owing to his long residence with Raṇajita Malla at Bhātgāon. The reverse is also a copy of the obverse of a coin of Yoga Prakāśa Malla of Pātan (Pl. VI, Fig. 3), and is similar to several of the later coins of both Kāṭhmāṇḍū and Pātan; even the two horizontal lines in the central circle being reproduced from the meaningless imitated Persian characters on those coins.

In the half mohars (*sukā*) and quarter mohars (*sukī*), too, the designs of the Newār coins were followed, and the same symbols, the sword and wreath as the emblem of sovereignty, the trident, the offering vase in form of *stūpa* (Pl. VII, Fig. 8), and the *cakra* on pedestal (Pl. VII, Fig. 8), were adopted. The lion, as a rebus for the name "Siṁha," was also used by Pratāpa Siṁha Sāha (No. 17; Pl. VII, Fig. 5, and others of his coins). The Malla coins from which the different Gorkhā coins were taken are noted in the List of Gorkhā Coins. The Gorkhā coins also bear the symbols of the Sun and Moon; as the Gorkhās claim to be descended from both the Solar and Lunar races.

In the gold coinage, however, the Gorkhā kings introduced coins of new denomination and of new designs, some examples of which are illustrated (Pl. VII, Figs. 4, 7, and 9). The copper coinage of Surendra Vikrama Sāha (Pl. VII, Fig. 11), and of Pṛthvī Vīra Vikrama Sāha (Pl. VII, Figs. 12 and 13) are new, with their devices, and in the latter a new symbol is introduced in the *Pādukā* (footprints of Viṣṇu) and the crossed *Kukhrīs*, the national Gorkhā weapon.

The names of deities also appear on the coins, though here the name of Gorkhānātha, the patron deity of the Gorkhās, is the one that is borne on all the mohars. But the name of Lokanātha also appears on some mohars of Pṛthvī Nārāyaṇa (No. 3) and that of Guhyesvarī on that of Pratāpa Siṁha Sāha, the name being spelt on the Gorkhā coins with *hy* instead of *jh* as on the Newār coins (No. 12). In the latter mohars, however, the only names that appear are those of Gorakhānātha and Bhavānī.

The Newār era was, however, abandoned. The coins of the Gorkhā kings are dated in the Sāka era, and the copper coins of Pṛthvī Vīra Vikrama Sāha in the Saṁvat era.

The Gorkhā kings all bear the title of Sāha Deva. The title of Sāha (Shāh) is said to have been conferred by the Emperor of Delhi on Jagdeva Khān, the forty-first king of the Gorkhā dynasty, for some service that he rendered to the emperor, and has been borne by all his successors.[1]

The different denominations of the Gorkhā silver coinage have already been considered. The gold coinage, however, comprises some further denominations. With the exception of Bakla, which is equivalent to two mohars, and of the gold mohar, which is known as 'Patlā' (thin coin) or 'Majhawālā' (middle coin), these gold coins, are not in general circulation. The smaller denominations are only minted on special occasions and for special purposes. For the names by which they are known, I am indebted to His Excellency Maharaja Sir Chandra Shamsher Jang Raṇa Bahadur, G.C.S.I., the Prime Minister of Nepal, who has kindly given me the information.

The gold coinage is nominally based on the standard of the tola (= 180 grains), the mohar being held to be the equivalent of half a tola. In the coins of the previous Gorkhā kings which I have weighed, however, the actual weights are less than that standard, as will be seen from the weights given in Table IV of Gorkhā coins. But I have not weighed any coins of the present reign. Their value generally fluctuates with the market price of gold. The different denominations are as follows :—

Duitola Asarfi,	made of	2	tolas	of gold	= 360	grs.,	actual weight	356 grs. ; coin No. 10.
Baklā	,,	1	,,	,,	= 180	,,	,, ,,	170 grs. ; coin No. 46.
Patlā or Mājhawālā	,,	$\frac{1}{2}$	,,	,,	= 90	,,		
Sukā Asarfi	,,	$\frac{1}{4}$	,,	,,	= 45	,,	,, ,,	41 or 42 gr. ; coins Nos. 25 and 47.
Sukī	,,	$\frac{1}{8}$	,,	,,	= 22·5	,,	,, ,,	21 grs. ; coin No. 22.
Ānī	,,	$\frac{1}{16}$	,,	,,	= 11·75	,,	,, ,,	11 grs. ; coin No. 27.
Ādhānī	,,	$\frac{1}{32}$	,,	,,	= 5·9	,,		
Pāi	,,	$\frac{1}{64}$	,,	,,	= 2·95	,,		
Dām	,,	$\frac{1}{256}$	,,	,,	= ·7	,,		
Phokā Dām	,,	$\frac{1}{512}$	,,	,,	= ·35	,,	,, ,,	·3 to ·35 gr. ; coin No. 77.

[1] Wright's History, p. 276.

A list of the different coins of the Gorkhā dynasty is given. It is complete up to coin No. 33, for the coins of the British Museum, and after that, I believe, contains most of the succeeding coins, though, owing to my leaving England, I had not the time to go through the remaining coins in the British Museum in detail; and the subsequent list is therefore compiled from the coins in my own collection, supplemented by those in the British Museum of which I had kept note, including those described by Marsden and also, in the case of coins Nos. 43 and 90, from the catalogue of coins in the India Museum, Calcutta. There may be other queens' coins, and also coins of other denominations than those contained in the list. But the present list will give a comprehensive idea of the Gorkhā coinage until the catalogue of these coins in the British Museum is published.

LISTS OF COINS.

THE LICCHAVI AND THĀKURĪ DYNASTIES.

MĀNĀṄKA OR MĀNADEVA.

No.	Metal. Weight. Size.	Obverse.	Reverse.
1	Æ 197 1·0	Lion walking towards left, with a flower in front of it. Over, in a straight line, legend *Śrī Mānāṅka*. (Pl. I, Fig. 1.)	Goddess seated on a lotus, with the right hand raised and the fingers spread out. The left hand rests on the hips. Legend, *Śrī Bhogini*.

The above coin, given in the British Museum, is Cunningham's coin figured in "Coins of Ancient India," pl. xiii, fig. 1.

The British Museum has twelve specimens of this type of coin and its varieties, which vary in size from ·95 to

1·05 and in weight. They vary considerably in workmanship, in the size of the seated figure, which in one specimen occupies the greater part of the obverse and in another not more than one-third of the diameter, in the details of the design, and in the workmanship, some being so much more barbarous that they would appear to be subsequent imitations of the original coinage. Cunningham's specimen is much the most perfect.

Cunningham and Bendall give the "deity seated on lotus throne" as the obverse of this coin, and the lion as the reverse. I do not think this is correct. The lion is, I think, the obverse, as it occurs on the obverse of Aṁśu-varman's coins, Pl. I, Figs. 5 and 6 (in which latter coin the obverse and reverse have, by mistake, been transposed on the plate), and on Jiṣṇu Gupta's coin, Pl. I, Fig. 8, in each of which there is no doubt, from the inscription, that the lion is the obverse. Cunningham describes the figure as "lion walking to left towards lotus plant with flower and bird." I think neither of the objects is a bird. The upper one is a flower consisting of six petals round a centre, and the lower one appears to be a lotus leaf. Bendall (coins Nos. 2, 3, 4, 5) describes the figure as "lion pawing a vine-branch," and mentions that Professor P. Gardner had called his attention to the Græco-Indian coin of Agathokles bearing a panther pawing a vine-leaf (Num. Chron. for 1868, vol. viii, pl. x). I do not think, however, that the object on the present coin is intended for a vine-branch. The upper object, if it were intended for a bunch of grapes, would be hanging down. Also grapes are not grown in Nepal, whereas flowers appear on many of these early Nepalese coins. I think there is no doubt that the object in front of the lion is intended for a lotus on a stem, from which a leaf also grows.

The figure of the deity seated on a lotus on the reverse bears so striking a resemblance to a similar figure on some of the coins of Huvishka as to suggest that it was copied from them. As already noted, Professor Bendall read the legend on the reverse of a coin of this type as *Śrī Bhaginī*. It is, however, distinctly *Śrī Bhoginī* on this and the other specimens in the British Museum.

No.	Metal. Weight. Size.	Obverse.	Reverse.
		GUṆĀṄKA OR GUṆA DEVA.	
2	Æ 165 ·95	Deity seated on a lotus, right hand held up. Legend below the figure. *Śrī Guṇāṅka.*	Elephant facing to right. (Pl. I, Fig. 2.)
3	Æ 130 ·87	Seated figure of king wearing crown; both hands are raised and holding a flower. Legend above the figure, *Śrī Guṇāṅka.*	Elephant to right, surrounded by margin of dots. (Pl. I, Fig. 3.)

The British Museum has twelve specimens of coin No. 2, which vary as greatly as those of Mānāṅka, and two of the variety shown in coin No. 3. In some the reverse is surrounded by a margin of dots, and in one specimen there is a scolloped line within the dots, enclosing each dot in a scollop, and in others a plain circle within the dots. The seated figure also varies considerably. In some specimens the figure occupies the lower part of the coin and sits on a throne, not on a flower, and is crowned, and appears to be a king rather than a deity.

No.	Metal. Weight. Size.	Obverse.	Reverse.
		VAIŚRAVAṆA.	
4	Æ 172 1·0	Seated figure, with right arm raised, holding a flower, left arm resting on thigh, a flower-pot to the left. The figure is crowned, and would appear to be a king. Legend, *Vaiśravaṇa.*	Cow facing to left, with calf underneath. Legend, *Kāmadehi.* (Pl. I, Fig. 4.) This sacred cow (Kāmadhenu) sprang from the churning of the ocean, and possessed the power of granting wishes.

The British Museum has three specimens of this type. They vary very little.

No.	Metal. Weight. Size.	Obverse.	Reverse.
		AMŚU-VARMAN (ṬHĀKURĪ DYNASTY).	
5	Æ 170 1·0	Winged lion facing left, with foot raised. Legend above, *Śryamśu Varma.*	Cow facing left, with calf underneath. Legend, *Kāmadehi.* (Pl. I, Fig. 5.)

The British Museum has ten specimens of this type. They vary very little

No.	Metal. Weight. Size.	Obverse.	Reverse.
6	Æ 228·5 1·0	In the centre the sun surrounded by rays. Legend running round, *Mahārājādhirājasya.*	Winged lion facing left, with foot raised. Legend, *Śryamśoḥ.* (Pl. I, Fig. 6.)

The British Museum has three specimens of this coin. They do not vary in design.

No.	Metal. Weight. Size.	Obverse.	Reverse.
7	Æ 155 ·95	Winged lion to left, with foot raised. Legend above, *Śryamśu Varma.*	Lion to left, with foot raised. Crescent over the lion. (Pl. I, Fig. 7.)

The British Museum has five specimens of this coin.

No.	Metal. Weight. Size.	Obverse.	Reverse.
		JISṆU GUPTA.	
8	Æ 174·5 ·95	Winged bull to left, with forefoot raised. Legend above, *Śrī Jiṣṇu Guptasya.*	Ornamental symbol. (Pl. I, Fig. 8.)

There is only one specimen of this coin in the British Museum.

The figure on the obverse of this coin is described by Cunningham as a winged lion, similar to the winged lions on the preceding coins. I think, however, that it is a winged bull. The shape of the head is quite different from that of the lions. The legs are thinner, and distinctly end in hoofs and not in paws. The shape of the quarters is square like those of a bull, while those of the lions are all round. The tail also is the tail of a bull and not of a lion.

No.	Metal. Weight. Size.	Obverse.	Reverse.

PAŚUPATI.

No.	Metal. Weight. Size.	Obverse.	Reverse.
9	Æ 105 ·85	Recumbent bull to left. Legend above, *Paśupati.*	Sun in the centre, surrounded by rays. (Pl. I, Fig. 9.)

The British Museum has five specimens of this coin. They vary in the size of the sun and the shape of the rays round it, but otherwise are similar.

No.	Metal. Weight. Size.	Obverse.	Reverse.
10	Æ 119 ·95	Similar to obverse of the preceding coin.	Symbol similar to that on obverse of coin No. 8 (Pl. I, Fig. 8), but smaller and not in high relief.

There is only one specimen of this coin in the British Museum, which is Cunningham's coin No. 9.

No.	Metal. Weight. Size.	Obverse.	Reverse.
11	Æ 97·5 ·90	Humped bull, standing to right, with crescent above.	Sun, with rays in centre. Round it legend *Paśupati.* (Pl. I, Fig. 10.)

There are nine specimens of this type in the British Museum.

No.	Metal. Weight. Size.	Obverse.	Reverse.
12	Æ 49 ·75	Similar to the preceding coin, but of half the weight and value.	Similar to the preceding.

There are ten specimens of this coin in the British Museum, ranging from 43 to 48 grains in weight according to their condition, and from ·75 to ·80 of an inch in size. They are all much worn.

No.	Metal. Weight. Size.	Obverse.	Reverse.
13	Æ 174 ·85	Humped bull, standing to left, with crescent above.	Similar to reverse of the preceding coin, but with a crescent with a dot inside it between each character of the legend *Paśupati.*
14	Æ 152 ·95	Humped bull, standing to left. Over it legend in one line, *Paśupati.*	Large sun in centre, surrounded by rays, similar to reverse of coin No. 9. (See Pl. I, Fig. 9 above.)

There are two specimens of this coin in the British Museum.

No.	Metal. Weight. Size.	Obverse.	Reverse.
15	Æ 163 ·9	Trident, with an axe attached to the shaft of it on the left, and some ornament hanging from it on the right. Legend, *Paśupati*.	Sun surrounded by rays. Round it legend *Paśupati*. (Pl. I, Fig. 11.)

There are two specimens in the British Museum.

No.	Metal. Weight. Size.	Obverse.	Reverse.
16	Æ — ·85	Trident, but with no axe or ornament attached to the shaft. Legend as in the preceding.	Sun surrounded by curved rays of the following form No legend.

There is one specimen only in the British Museum.

No.	Metal. Weight. Size.	Obverse.	Reverse.
17	Æ — 1·0	Design similar to obverse of coin No. 11 (Fig. 10). Legend, *Paśu* and two dots in the place of the other two characters.	Design similar to obverse of coin No. 11 (Fig. 10). Legend, *Pati* and two dots occupying the place of the other two characters.

There is one specimen in the British Museum.

No.	Metal. Weight. Size.	Obverse.	Reverse.
18	Æ 116 ·90	Seated figure of king on a high-backed throne, wearing a crown, right hand raised, left hand bent and resting on thigh, flower to left springing from below foot, vase of flowers to right.	Vase of flowers, with legend *Paśupati* in one line.
19	Æ 146 ·85	Seated figure of a king wearing a crown, with his right hand resting on the knee and left arm bent resting on the hips.	Similar to the reverse of the preceding coin. (Pl. I, Fig. 12.)
20	Æ 116 ·9	Seated figure of a king wearing a crown, with right hand raised and fingers extended, left hand extended resting on knee and holding a flower.	Vase of flowers with an ornamental scroll or a flowering branch on each side of it. Legend in two lines, *Paśupati*. (Pl. I, Fig. 13.)

THE MALLA DYNASTY.

Kingdom of Bhātgāon.

No.	Metal. Weight. Size.	Date. A.D.	Obverse.	Reverse.
			JAGATPRAKĀŚA MALLA.	
1	Æ 85 1·05	1632	Three-lined legend in scolloped square, *Śrī Śrī Jagatprakāśa Malla*; above the square, figure of hand-drum (*damaru*), and below, date 752 N.S.; on either side imitation of Arabic characters upside down.	*Triśula* (trident) with ornamental scroll attached within central circle; above it sword with wreath; around, imitation of Arabic characters upside down. British Museum. (Pl. II, Fig. 1.)
			JAYA JITAMITRA MALLA.	
2	Æ 90 1·1	1663	Three-lined legend in scolloped square, *Śrī Śrī Jaya Jitamitra Malla*; outside the square, imitation Arabic characters upside down as in the preceding; date below, 783 N.S.	Similar to preceding. (Pl. II, Fig. 2.)
			JAYA BHŪPATĪNDRA MALLA.	
3	Æ 80 1·02	1696	Three-lined legend in scolloped square, *Śrī Śrī Jaya Bhūpatīndra Malla Deva*. Around, characters similar to preceding. Date, 816 N.S.	Similar to preceding. (Pl. II, Fig. 3.)
4	Æ 21 ·7 (pierced coin)	1696	(Quarter mohar.) Dagger and wreath within two intersecting squares; above, two crescents and stars; legend, *Śrī Śrī Jaya Bhūpa-*.	Vase of holy water, *kalaśa*, with streamers. The ornament on the top of the vase is obliterated by the piercing of the coin; above, two crescents and stars; legend, *tīndra Malladeva*; date below, 816 N.S. (Pl. II, Fig. 5.)

JAYA RAṆAJITA MALLA.

No.	Metal. Weight. Size.	Date. A.D.	Obverse.	Reverse.
5	Æ 83·5 1·1	1722	Similar to No. 1. Three-lined legend, *Śrī Śrī Jaya Raṇajita Malla Deva*; below, date 842 N.S.	Similar to No. 1. (Pl. II, Fig. 4.)
6	Æ 84 1·05	1722	In central circle, shell, lotus, and *cakra*; on margin to r. a bow, to l. five arrows; floral ornaments round; legend, *Śrī Śrī Jaya Raṇa-*.	In centre a triangular *bāṇāstra* (conventional bow and arrow); within it a (*pāśa*) noose and (*aṅkuśa*) elephant goad; around it, to r. a *chāmara* (yak's tail fly-whisk), to l. a lotus; flower ornaments. Legend, *Jita Malla Deva*. Date below, 842 N.S. (Pl. II, Fig. 8.) *Note.*—This coin is a copy of Jaya Cakravartīndra's coin No. 15.
7	Æ 41·5 ·92	1722	(Half mohar.) Continuous-lined figure forming five triangles on the sides of a pentagon; in pentagon, sword and wreath, two suns and legend *Śrī Śrī*; in triangles, *Jaya Raṇa Ji-*; in spaces round, *-ta Malla Deva*.	In *bāṇāstra* triangle vase of holy water, *kalaśa*, with streamers and two crescents and dots. Round, date *Vaiśākha* 15 *Saṁvat*. 842. (Pl. II, Fig. 7.) *Note.* — The obverse and reverse of this coin are transposed on the Plate.
8	Æ (pierced coin) 21 ·67	1722	(Quarter mohar.) Similar to No. 4. Quarter mohar of Bhūpatīndra. Legend, *Śrī Śrī Jaya Raṇa-*.	Similar to No. 4. Legend, *-jita Malla Deva*; date, 842 N.S. (Pl. II, Fig. 6.)

No.	Metal. Weight. Size.	Date. A.D.	Obverse.	Reverse.
9	AR (–) ·56	No date.	(Quarter.) Sword without wreath; two crescents and stars. Legend in three lines, *Srī Śrī Jaya Raṇa-*.	Legend in three lines, (1) *Jita*, (2) *Malla De*, (3) *va*. No date. British Museum. (Not figured.)

Kingdom of Kāṭhmāṇḍū.

LAKSMĪNARA SIṀHA.

No.	Metal. Weight. Size.	Date. A.D.	Obverse.	Reverse.
10	AR 70·5 1·05	No date.	Similar to reverse of No. 1, but with legend *Srī* in place of sword and wreath. No date. (Pl. II, Fig. 9.)	In square a shell and two-lined legend, *Śrī Lakṣmī Nara Sim.* Characters round the square similar to the obverse of No. 1. *Note.*—The obverse and reverse of this coin are transposed on the Plate for continuity with coins Nos. 1, 2, 3, and 4.

PRATĀPA MALLA.

No.	Metal. Weight. Size.	Date. A.D.	Obverse.	Reverse.
11	AR 77 1·03	1641	Similar to the preceding coin of Lakṣmīnara Siṁha. Legend, *Śrī Pratāpa Malla*. Date, 761 N.S.	Similar to the preceding coin of Lakṣmīnara Siṁha. (Pl. II, Fig. 10.) *Note.*—The obverse and reverse are transposed on the Plate, as in the preceding coin.
12	AR 87 1·02	1656	Imitation Persian characters in two lines, intended for '*San Ilahi*'; in centre, trident; the ground covered with flowers. Legend, *Śrī Śrī Kavīndra Jaya*.	Imitation Persian characters in two lines, *Jahangir Shah*; ground covered with flowers. Legend, *Pratāpa Malla*. Date, 776 N.S. (Pl. II, Fig. 12.)

No.	Metal. Weight. Size.	Date. A.D.	Obverse.	Reverse.
13	Æ 171 1·05	1661	(Double mohar.) A square coin; in ornamental square surrounded by floral margin. Trident with legend, *Śrī 2. Rāja Rājendra Jaya.*	In ornamental square surrounded by floral margin; sword and legend, *Pratāpa Malla Deva.* Date, 781 N.S. (Pl. II, Fig. 14.) This coin, which is unique, belongs to Dr. Hoernle. It is perhaps a *nisār.*

RŪPAMATĪ DEVĪ.

No.	Metal. Weight. Size.	Date. A.D.	Obverse.	Reverse.
14	Æ 21·5 ·72	1649	(Quarter mohar.) Trident; two crescents and stars. Legend, *Śrī Rūpamatī.*	Imitation Persian characters in two lines on floral ground; two crescents and stars. Legend, *Devī.* Date, 769 N.S. British Museum. (Pl. II, Fig. 11.)

JAYA CAKRAVARTĪNDRA MALLA.

No.	Metal. Weight. Size.	Date. A.D.	Obverse.	Reverse.
15	Æ 82 1·02	1669	In central circle, shell, lotus, and *cakra*; on margin, to r. a bow, to l. five arrows; floral ornaments round. Legend, *Śrī. 2 Jaya Cakra Va-.*	In triangular *bāṇāstra* (conventional bow and arrow) a noose and elephant goad; around it, to r. *chāmara* (yak's tail fly-whisk), to l. lotus; and, on floral ground, legend *rtīndra Malla.* Date, 789 N.S. (Pl. II, Fig. 13.)

JAYA NRPENDRA MALLA.

No.	Metal. Weight. Size.	Date. A.D.	Obverse.	Reverse.
16	Æ 80 1·0	1675	Imitation Persian characters in two lines; in centre, trident; above, sun; flowered field. Legend, *Śrī Śrī Jaya Nṛpendra.*	Imitation Persian characters in two lines; in centre, sword and wreath; above, crescent; flowered field. Legend, *Malla Deva.* Date, 795 N.S (Pl. III, Fig. 1.)

No.	Metal. Weight. Size.	Date. A.D.	Obverse.	Reverse.
			JAYA PĀRTHIVENDRA MALLA. (Queen Rājya Lakṣmī Devī.)	
17	AR 87 1·05	1682	Two intersecting squares. In central octagon, legend *Śrī Śrī Jaya Pārthivendra Malla Deva.* In the triangles round, legend *Ma-hā-rā-ja-Ne-pā-le-nd'ra.* In the angles outside the figure, the *aṣṭa-maṅgala* (eight emblems of the Buddhist religion).	Two intersecting squares. In centre, vase of holy water, *kalaśa*, and wreath on a lotus. Legend, *Rājya Lakṣmī Devī.* Date, 802 N.S. In the eight triangles, legend *Mahārāṇī Jagatmālā.* Around, in each of the outer angles, a flower. (Pl. III, Fig. 2.)
18	AR 84 1·0	1680	Imitation Persian characters in two lines. In centre, trident; to l., shell; to r., *kalaśa*; above, sun. Legend on flowered field, *Śrī Śrī Jaya Pārthivendra.*	Imitation Persian characters in two lines. In centre, shell to l.; two crossed yak's tail fly-whisks; to r., the symbol of the two golden fishes. Legend on flowered field, *Malla Deva.* Below, date 800 N.S. British Museum. (Pl. III, Fig. 3.)
19	AR (–) ·70	No date.	(Quarter mohar.) In centre, trident and two crescents and stars. Legend in five lines: (1) *Śrī*, (2) *Jaya*, (3) *Pārthi*, (4) *vendra*, (5) *Malla.*	Offering vase and wreath. Legend in four lines: (1) *Śrī*, (2) *Rājya*, (3) *Lakṣmī*, (4) *Devī.* (Not figured.)
			JAYA BHŪPĀLENDRA MALLA.	
20	AR 87·5 1·07	1692	Within circle, trident and two crescents and stars. Legend, *Śrī* 2, *Jaya Bhūpālendra Malla.* Round circle, in eight lotus petals, the *aṣṭa-maṅgala.*	Within scolloped octagon, sword and wreath, and legend *Malla Deva.* Date, 812 N.S. Round the figure, in eight leaves, legend *Nepāleśvara Rājendra.* (Pl. III, Fig. 4.)

No.	Metal. Weight. Size.	Date. A.D.	Obverse.	Reverse.
21	Æ 87 1·07	1700	Design similar to preceding. Legend in circle, *Śrī 2, Vīra Bhūpālendra*. Round circle, in eight lotus petals, *Girīndra Rāja Rājendra*.	Design similar to preceding. In circle, legend *Srī Śrī Kavi-*; in leaves round *ndra, Chuḍāmaṇi Samrāṭ*. Date, 812 N.S. (Not figured.)

JAYA BHĀSKARA MALLA.

No.	Metal. Weight. Size.	Date. A.D.	Obverse.	Reverse.
22	Æ 85 1·07	1701	Similar to coin (No. 20) of Bhūpālendra. In circle, legend *Śrī Śrī Jaya Bhāskara*.	In circle, imitation Persian characters in two lines; in centre, sword and wreath. In circle, legend *Malla Deva*. Date, 821 N.S. In eight trefoil leaves round, *Nepāleśvara Girīndra*. (Pl. III, Fig. 5.)
23	Æ 21 (pierced coin) ·70	1698	(Quarter mohar.) Persian characters in two lines. In centre, trident; above, crescent. Legend, *Śrī 2, Jaya Bhāskara*.	Persian characters in two lines. In centre, shell. Legend, *Malla Deva*. Date, 818 N.S. (Pl. III, Fig. 6.)

JAYA VĪRA MAHĪNDRA MALLA.

No.	Metal. Weight. Size.	Date. A.D.	Obverse.	Reverse.
24	Æ 85 1·02	1709	In circle, trident and legend *Śrī Śrī*, and date 829 N.S. Around, in six scolloped petals, legend *Jaya Vīra Mahīndra Malla*.	In circle, sword and wreath, sun and moon. Around, in six scolloped petals. *Śrī Śrī Lokanātha nama* (worship to Loknath). (Pl. III, Fig. 7.)
25	Æ 86·5 1·05	1717	In circle, trident and legend *Śrī Śrī Jaya Mahīndra*. Around, in leaves, *aṣṭa-maṅgala*.	In circle, sword and wreath, and legend *Siṁha Deva*. Date, 837 N.S. Around, in eight leaves, *Śrī Śrī Śrī Kaluṇāmaya*. (Pl. III, Fig. 8.)

No.	Metal. Weight. Size.	Date. A.D.	Obverse.	Reverse.
26	Æ 82 1·05	1716	In circle, trident and legend *Śrī Śrī Jaya Mahīndra*. Around, in petals, *aṣṭa-maṅgalā*.	In circle, sword and wreath, and Arabic characters. Legend, *Siṁha Deva*. Date, 836 N.S. Around, in eight petals, *Nepāleśvara Girīndra*. (Pl. III, Fig. 9.)
27	Æ 20·5 ·66	1718	(Quarter mohar.) Trident, and two crescents and stars. Legend, *Śrī 2, Jaya Mahīndra Siṁha Deva*.	Offering vase and wreath. Legend, *Śrī Mahīndra Lakṣmī*. Date, 838 N.S. (Pl. III, Fig. 10.)
	JAYA JAGAJJAYA, *alias* MAHĪPATENDRA SIṀHA. (Queen Kumudinī Devī.)			
28	Æ 85 1·1	1732	In circle, trident; around, *aṣṭa-maṅgala*. Similar to Nos. 20, 22, 25, and 26. Legend, *Śrī 2, Jaya Jagajjaya*.	Similar to No. 26. In circle, legend *Malla Deva*. Around, in eight leaves, *Nepāleśvara Rājendra*. Date, 852 N.S. (Pl. III, Fig. 11.)
29	Æ 80 1·1	1738	Design similar to the preceding. Legend, *Śrī 2, Jagajjaya Malla*.	In octagon, sword and wreath. Legend, *Śrī 2. Mahīpatīndra Malla*. Date, 858 N.S. (Pl. III, Fig. 12.)
30	Æ 19·5 67	1732	(Quarter mohar.) Trident, and two crescents and stars and crescent above. Legend, *Śrī 2, Jaya Jagajjaya Malla*.	Offering vase and wreath. Legend, *Śrī Kumudinī Devī*. Date, 852 N.S. (Pl. III, Fig. 13.)
31	Æ (–) 1·0	No date.	Within lozenge, trident; around, in four compartments and on field, legend *Śrī Jaya Mahīpa*.	Sword and wreath; two crescents and stars, on flowered field. Legend in three lines, *-tīndra Malla Deva*. No date. British Museum. (Pl. IV, Fig. 1.)

JAYA PRAKĀŚA MALLA.

(QUEEN DOWAGER (?), KUMUDINĪ DEVĪ.)

No.	Metal. Weight. Size.	Date. A.D.	Obverse.	Reverse.
32	Æ 82·5 1·07	1756	Design similar to Nos. 20, 22, 25, 26, 28, and 29. Legend, *Śrī 2, Jaya Prakāśa Malla*.	Design similar to No. 29. In centre, legend *Śrī 2, Mahīpatīndra Malla*. Date, 876 N.S. (Pl. IV, Fig. 2.) The form of the figure 7, ʅ, on this coin and on coins Nos. 37 and 39, is unusual on the Malla coins, and on other coins of Jaya Prakāśa, viz. coins Nos. 38, 40, and 45, it is in the usual form, ∩.
33	Æ 65·5 1·10	—	Barbarous imitation of the preceding.	Barbarous imitation of the preceding. Base metal. Marsden, MCX. British Museum. (Pl. IV, Fig. 3.)
34	Æ 70 1·10	—	Barbarous imitation of No. 31.	Barbarous imitation of No. 31. Marsden, MCXI. Very base metal. British Museum. (Pl. IV, Fig. 4.)
35	Æ 82·5 1·10	1753	In scolloped octagon, a trident, beneath it a crouching lion. Legend, *Śrī 2, Jaya Prakāśa Malla*; around, in petals, *asta-mangala*.	Within a circle a triangular *bāṇāstra*; round it, within circle, sword and wreath, sun and moon, and date 873 N.S.; around, in petals, *Śrī 2, Mahīpatīndra Malla*. (Pl. IV, Fig. 5.)

No.	Metal. Weight. Size.	Date. A.D.	Obverse.	Reverse.
36	Æ 83 1·12	1753	Within pointed octagon, trident and legend, *Śrī* 2, *Jaya Prakāśa Malla*. Around, in petals, *asṭa-maṅgala*; between petals, legend *Nepāleśvara* and date 873 N.S.	Within scolloped circle, triangle in centre, and round it legend *Śrī* 3 *Taleju Māju*. Around, in petals, *Śrī Śrī Śrī Kumārī*; outside these, legend *Śrī Mahīpatīndra Malla*. (Pl. IV, Fig. 6.)
37	Æ 21·6 ·67	1755	(Half mohar.) Within circle, trident and two crescents and stars. Around, in four trefoils, *Śrī* 2, *Jaya Pra-*.	Two lines intended for Arabic characters. In centre, sword and wreath. Legend, *kāśa Malla Deva*. Date, 875. Marsden, MCXIII. British Museum. (Pl. IV, Fig 7.)
38	Æ 42·2 ·90	1753	(Half mohar.) Within, scolloped lozenge, a trident, with two flowers growing from its shaft. Around, four petals; within, petals; and on intervening spaces, legend *Śrī* 2, *Jaya Prakāśa Malla*.	Within circle, sword and wreath. Around, in four petals, legend *Deva*, and date 873 N.S. British Museum. (Pl. IV, Fig. 8.)
39	Æ	1756	(Quarter mohar.) In centre, trident. Legend, *Śrī Jananī Ku-*.	In centre, *cakra* on pedestal. Legend, *-mudinī Devī*. Date, 876 N.S. Marsden, MCXIV. British Museum. (Pl. IV, Fig. 9.)
40	Æ 18·6 ·70	1753	(Quarter mohar.) In centre, trident, above to l., figure of hand-drum (*damaru*). Legend, *Śrī* 3, *Paśupati*.	In centre, sword and wreath. Legend, *Śrī* 3, *Gujheśvarī*. Date, 873 N.S. British Museum. (Pl. IV, Fig. 10.)
41	Æ 21 ·72	1753	(Quarter mohar.) Trident only. Legend, *Śrī* 2, *Jaya Prakāśa Malla*.	Similar to preceding. (Pl. IV, Fig. 11.)

No.	Metal. Weight. Size.	Date. A.D.	Obverse.	Reverse.
42	Æ 5·75 ·45	No date.	(Sixteenth of a mohar.) Sword and wreath, on a pedestal. Legend, *Śrī Jaya Prakā-*.	Small crouching lion with tail raised forward over body; above, legend *-śa Malla*. British Museum. (Pl. IV, Fig. 13.)
43	Æ 2·75 ·35	No date.	(Thirty-secondth of a mohar.) Sword. Legend, *Śrī Jaya Pra-*.	The coin a thin leaf of silver, and is only stamped on the obverse. (Pl. IV, Fig. 14.)

Gold Coinage.

No.	Metal. Weight. Size.	Date. A.D.	Obverse.	Reverse.
44	AV 84·5 1·15	No date.	(Ashrafi.) An exact copy in gold of coin No. 36.	An exact copy of coin No. 36. (*Cf.* Pl. IV, Fig. 6.) British Museum.
45	AV 21 67	No date.	(Quarter ashrafi.) Trident. Legend, *Jaya Prakāśa Malla*.	Sword and wreath Legend. *Śrī Gujheśvarī*; date, 873 N.S. British Museum (Pl. IV, Fig. 12.)
46	AV 5·0 ·47	No date.	Same as silver coin No. 42.	Same as No. 42.
47	AV 2·0 ·45	No date.	Similar to the preceding.	Nothing stamped. Thin gold leaf; the obverse stamping shows through.
48	AV	No date.	Same as silver coin No. 43.	Same as No. 43.

JYOTI PRAKĀŚA MALLA.

(*Coin struck during a rebellion.*)

No.	Metal. Weight. Size.	Date. A.D.	Obverse.	Reverse.
49	Æ 98 1·1	1746	Similar to No. 32 of Jaya Prakāśa. Legend, *Śrī Jyoti Prakāśa Malla*.	Similar to No. 32. Legend in octagon, *Śrī Śrī Mahipatīndra Malla*. Date, 866 N.S. (Pl. IV, Fig. 15.)

No.	Metal. Weight. Size.	Date. A.D.	Obverse.	Reverse.
			(JANANĪ) JAYA LAKṢMĪ DEVĪ. (Queen Mother of Jyoti Prakāśa Malla.) (*Coin struck in a rebellion.*)	
50	Æ 18 65	1746	(Quarter mohar.) Trident with flower above, and two crescents and dots. Legend, *Śrī Jananī.*	Offering vase with covering in form of *stūpa,* and wreath, with crescent above. Legend, *Jaya Lakṣmī Devī.* Date, 866 N.S. (Pl. VI, Fig. 12.) *Note.*—This coin was, by oversight, omitted from Pl. IV. It is shown on the last plate of Malla coins. The obverse is figured below the reverse.
			KINGDOM OF PĀTAN OR LALITAPUR. **SIDDHI NARASIṀHA.**	
51	Æ 85·5 1·1	1631	Within central circle, sword and crescent. Legend, *Śrī Śrī Siddhi.* Around, imitation Arabic characters upside down, as on the obverse of coins No. 1, 2, 3, 5, 9, and 10, but with a flower above in place of the sword and wreath.	Within central circle, a lion to r. Around, imitation Arabic characters upside down, similar to those on the obverse of coins Nos. 1, etc., but with a flower to l., and above two crescents and dots, and legend *Nara,* making with the lion in the centre *Nara-'siṁha.'* Below, date 751 N.S. (Pl. V, Fig. 1.)
52	Æ 20·5 ·7	1654	(Quarter mohar.) Sword, flower, and two crescents and dots. Legend, *Śrī Śrī Siddhi.*	Lion to r.; above legend, *Nara,* making with lion *Nara-'siṁha.'* Date, 774. (Pl. V, Fig. 2.)

No.	Metal. Weight. Size.	Date. A.D.	Obverse.	Reverse.
			JAYA ŚRINIVASA MALLA.	
53	Æ 81 ·96	1661	Characters as in No. 49, etc. In central circle, legend *Śrī Śrī Jaya.*	Characters with flower to right as in No. 49. Legend above, *Śrī Ni-*, within circle *vāsa Malla*. Below, date 781 N.S. (Pl. V, Fig. 3.)
54	Æ 86 1·03	1666	Two intersecting triangles. In centre, sword and wreath, flower, and two crescents and dots. Legend, in centre, *Śrī Śrī Jaya*; round in the six triangles, *Śrīnivāsa Malla.*	In central circle two *kalaśas* with streamers, with staff between and two small indistinct symools. Round it a square figure with projections from the sides. In the four corners of the figure two royal banners, a *cakra*, and a flower. Legend, *Nepāleśvara*. Date within circle, 786 N.S. (Pl. V, Fig. 4.)
			YOGA NARENDRA MALLA.	
55	Æ 83 ·98	1688	Figure formed of two interlaced svastikas. In the central square thus formed, sword; in the top and central squares, legend *Śrī* 3. *Lokanātha*. Legend commencing from top left corner and reading horizontally across *Śrī Śrī Yoga Narendra Malla Deva.* Outside the figure, legend *Saṁgītārṇṇavapāraga*, "Skilled in the flood of concerted music." *Note.*—This legend is misread in the recent Catalogue of the Coins in the India Museum, Calcutta, as *Saṁgī* (which has no meaning) *tāṇḍava pāraga*, "Skilled in the *tāṇḍava* (dance or mantra)."	Two intersecting quadrilaterals with concave sides. In central octagon so formed, circle surrounded by eight petals. Inside circle, vase of offerings with cover in form of *stūpa*, and wreath. In the eight triangles, legend *Śrī Yoga Lakṣmī Devī*. In the spaces outside the figure, legend *Śrī Narendra Lakṣmī Devī*. In bottom triangle, date 808 N.S. (Pl. V, Fig. 5.)

No.	Metal. Weight. Size.	Date A.D.	Obverse.	Reverse.
56	Æ ·85 1·02	1686	Similar to the preceding.	A rhomboid intersected by two equilateral triangles. In central rhomboid so formed, on pedestal, a vase for offerings with cover in form of *stūpa* and wreath; to l. shell, to r. mace. Within the larger rhomboid, legend *Śrī Narendra Lakṣmī Devī*. Outside the figure and in the bottom triangle, legend *Śrī Pratāpa Lakṣmī Devī*. At bottom, date 806 N.S. (Pl. V, Fig. 6.)
57	Æ 81·5 1·02	1685	Similar to the two preceding coins.	A smaller square, inscribed within another. Within, smaller square, vase of holy water, *kalaśa*, resting on a lotus; to l. shell, to r. standard; below these, to l. mace, to r. lotus. In triangles, to l. vase for offerings, to r. standard. Legend, *Yoga Lakṣmī Devī*. Date, 805 N.S. British Museum. (Pl. V, Fig. 7.)
58	Æ 81 1·1	1686	Small square inscribed within a larger. Round these, two intersecting squares. In the central square, sword. In the two central squares, legend *Śrī Śrī Śrī Lokanātha*. Within the figure of the intersecting squares, crescent and sun, and legend *Śrī Śrī Yoga Narendra Malla Deva*. Outside the figure, legend *Saṃgītārṇava-pāraga*. (See coin No. 55.)	Light pointed figure. In central octagon, vase for offerings and wreath, crescent and sun, shell and mace. Around, within the triangles, legend *Śrī Śrī Narendra Lakṣmī Devī*. Outside the figure, legend *Nepāla Chudāmaṇi*. Date, 806 N.S. (Pl. V, Fig. 8.)

No.	Metal. Weight. Size.	Date. A.D.	Obverse.	Reverse.
59	Æ 82 1·0	1700	In centre, on pedestal, sword with wreath; above, flower, crescent, and sun. Legend in five lines, in inner columns of characters, *Śrī Śrī Jaya Yoga Narendra Malla*. Legend in four lines in outer two columns, *Saṁgītārṇṇava-pāraga*. (See coin No. 55.)	In centre, trident resting on lotus. Legend in five lines of the two inner columns of characters, *Śrī Śrī Vīra Yoga Narendra Malla*. Legend in four lines forming outer columns, *Nepāleśvara Chuḍāmaṇi*. Date, 820 N.S. (Pl. V, Fig. 9.)
60	Æ 21 ·75	1687	(Quarter mohar.) A square with four trefoiled petals round. In square, staff, and legend *Śrī Śrī Yoga*, and date 807 N.S. Legend formed by the central characters of the top and lateral trefoils, *Narendra* (in lower trefoil) *Malla*; outer characters of top and lateral trefoils, *Dayā kara*, "Have pity," and letters *pa-pa* (or possibly *ya-ya*) in the lateral trefoils, and *ga* in the bottom trefoil, the meaning of which is not clear.	Five-pointed figure formed of a continuous line. In top three triangles and centre, legend *Śrī Śrī Śrī Lokanātha*; around and in two lower triangles, legend *Taleju Sahāya*, "Taleju's aid." (Pl V, Fig. 10.)
			JAYA INDRA MALLA.	
61	Æ 83 1·02	1706	In square, sword and wreath, with small *kalaśa* above and legend *Śrī Śrī Lokanātha*; outside, legend *Śrī Śrī Jaya Indra Malla*.	In square, figure with circularly projecting sides, trident resting on lotus; to l. *cakra* on pedestal; to r. vase for offerings with cover in form of *stūpa*. Legend, *Śrī Bhāgavatī Devī*, and date 826 N.S. (Pl. V, Fig. 11.)

No.	Metal. Weight. Size.	Date. A.D.	Obverse.	Reverse.
			YOGAMATĪ, (?) Widow of Yoga Narendra, with her son, LOKA PRAKAŚA MALLA.	
			(Coin taken from the Catalogue of Coins in the Indian Museum, Calcutta.)	
62	Æ 82·5 1·02	1707	"Square, with smaller square inscribed diagonally, and, in centre, a third square containing sword with wreath. Outer legend, *Śrī 2, Jaya Lokaprakāśa Malla Deva*; inner legend, *Śrī Śrī Kalunāmaya*."	"Two interlaced equilateral triangles, with central scolloped compartment, containing trident. Legend, *Śrī, Śrī Yogamatī Devī*; date below, 827 N.S. (= 1707 A.D.)." C.C.I.M.C., 1906, vol. i, p. 288.
			YOGAMATĪ, (?) Widow of Yoga Narendra, with her son, VĪRA NARASIṀHA MALLA.	
63	Æ 83 1·02	1709	Square, with semi-elliptical figure on each side. In square, dagger and wreath, crescent and sun, and legend *Śrī 2, Lokanātha*; outside and in the semi-elliptical figures, legend *Śrī Śrī Vīra Narasiṁha Mala Deva.*	An equilateral triangle inscribed within another; in lateral triangles, in l. *cakra* on pedestal, in r. vase of offerings; outside and in top triangle, legend *Śrī Śrī Yogamatī Devī*, and date 829 N.S. British Museum. (Pl. V, Fig. 12.)
			HṚDI NARASIṀHA MALLA.	
64	Æ 85 1·1	1716	In centre, circle surrounded by six trefoiled petals; outside this, quadrangular figure with projections from the sides. In circle, lion to l. with paw raised. Legend, in petals, *Śrī Śrī Hṛdi Nara*; in centre, lion = '*Siṁha*'; in corners of figure, *Mala Deva*.	Two intersecting equilateral triangles. In central figure, sword and wreath, crescent and sun, and *pāduka*. In petals and triangles of the figure, legend *Śrī Śrī Karuṇāmaya*. Date, 836 N.S. (Pl. VI, Fig. 1.)

No.	Metal. Weight. Size.	Date. A.D.	Obverse.	Reverse.
65	Æ 83·5 1·09	1716	Circle surrounded by six trefoiled petals, these again surrounded by six bifoiled petals. In circle, lion to l. with flower and stalk in front. Legend (in both series of petals together), *Śrī Śrī Vīra Hṛdi Nara* (lion in centre =) *Siṁha, Mala* (misspelt) *Deva*.	Circle surrounded by six unifoiled petals, these again surrounded by six trefoiled petals. Legend (in both series of petals together). *Śrī Śrī Karuṇāmaya Nama* and date 836 N.S. (Pl. VI, Fig. 2.)

JAYA YOGA PRAKĀŚA MALLA.

No.	Metal. Weight. Size.	Date. A.D.	Obverse.	Reverse.
66	Æ 83·5 1·1	1712	Circle surrounded by eight petals. In circle, trident and imitation Persian characters in two lines. Legend, (in circle) *Śrī Śrī Jaya Yo-*, (in petals) *-ga Prakāśa Malla Deva*. Date, 832 N.S. (Pl. VI, Fig. 3.)	Octagon with concave sides. In centre, resting on lotus, sword and wreath, crescent and sun, and flower on either side. Around, in eight lotus leaves, legend *Śrī Śrī Śrī Karunamaya* (misspelt *n* for *ṇ*). (Pl. VI, Fig. 3.)

JAYA VIṢṆU MALLA.

No.	Metal. Weight. Size.	Date. A.D.	Obverse.	Reverse.
67	Æ 83 1·07	1741	On reticulated surface; in centre, trident, imitation Persian characters in two lines, crescent and sun. Legend, *Śrī Śrī Jaya Viṣṇu Malla Deva*. Date, 861 N.S.	Scolloped circle. Within circle, sword and wreath on pedestal, and legend *Śrī Śrī Śrī Lokanātha* Outside the figure, reading across from side to side, legend *Śrī Jaya Vīra Yoga Narendra Malla Deva*. (Pl. V) Fig. 4.)

No.	Metal. Weight. Size.	Date. A.D.	Obverse.	Reverse.
68	Æ 82·5 1·05	1739	Circle surrounded by four petals. In circle, trident; in petals, umbrella, mace, flower, and *chakra*. Legend, (in circle) *Śrī Śrī*, (in petals) *Jaya Viṣṇu Malla Deva*. Date, 859 N.S.	In centre, sword and wreath, imitation Persian characters in two lines, two crescents and dots, and trailing flowers. Legend, *Śrī Śrī Śrī Karuṇāmaya*. (Pl. VI, Fig. 5.)

JAYA RĀJYA PRAKĀŚA MALLA.

No.	Metal. Weight. Size.	Date. A.D.	Obverse.	Reverse.
69	Æ 82 1·1	1736	In centre, trident, imitation Persian characters in two lines, crescent and sun. Legend, *Śrī Śrī Jaya Rājya Prakāśa Deva*. Date, 856 N.S.	Design as in No. 67 of *Jaya Viṣṇu Malla*. Legend, in scolloped circle, *Śrī Śrī Śrī Lokanātha*; outside, *Śrī Jaya Vīra Yoga Narendra Malla Deva*. (A very debased coin.) (Pl. VI, Fig. 6.)
70	Æ 82·5 1·05	1736	Circle in centre, round it a square with projections of double-key pattern. In circle, trident and sun. Legend, (in circle) *Śrī* 2, *Jaya Rājya*, (in outer figure) *Prakāśa Malla Deva*. Date, 856 N.S.	Design similar to preceding. Legend, (within scolloped circle) *Śrī Śrī Śrī Lokanātha*, (outside) *Śrī Jaya Vīra Yoga Narendra Malla Deva*. (Pl. VI, Fig. 7.)
71	Æ 82·5 1·08	1736	Two intersecting quadrilateral figures with concave sides. In centre, trident, crescent, and sun; outside, in the angles of the figure, the *Asta Mangala*. Legend, (in centre) *Śrī Śrī Jaya Rā-*, (round, in triangles) *-jya Prakāśa Malla Deva*. Date, 856 N.S.	Design same as Nos. 67, 69, and 70. Legend, (within scolloped circle) *Śrī Śrī Śrī Lokanātha*, (outside) *Śrī Jaya Vīra Yoga Narendra Malla Deva*. (Pl. VI, Fig. 8.)

No.	Metal. Weight. Size.	Date. A.D.	Obverse.	Reverse.
72	AR 84 1·2	1736	Octagon surrounded by eight petals. In octagon, trident with crescent on the shaft. Legend, (in octagon) *Śrī Śrī Śrī Hara Siddhi.* "The success of Hara. (in petals) *Śrī 2, Rājya Prakāśa Malla.* Date, 869 N.S.	Circle surrounded by eight petals. In circle, sword and sword on pedestal. Legend, (in circle) *Śrī Śrī Śrī Lokanātha.* (in petals) *Śrī 2. Yoga Narendra Malla.* British Museum. (Pl. VI, Fig. 9.)
			JAYA VIŚVAJITA MALLA.	
73	AR 82·5 1·08	1758	Circle surrounded by six petals, which are again surrounded by six scolloped petals. In circle, trident, crescent, and sun, and legend *Śrī Hara Siddhi*; in petals, *Śrī Śrī Jaya Viśvajita Malla Deva.* Date, 878 N.S.	Circle surrounded by eight lotus petals. In circle, sword and wreath on pedestal, and legend *Śrī Śrī Śrī Lokanātha*; in petals, *Śrī 2. Yoga Narendra Malla.* (Pl. VI, Fig. 10.)
74	AR 21 70	1752	(Quarter mohar.) Circle surrounded by six petals, in circle. Legend, (in circle) *Śrī*, (in petals) *Viśvajita Malla Deva.* Date (in circle), 872 N.S.	Circle surrounded by six petals. In circle, sword and wreath, two crescents and dots, and two lotus buds; in petals, legend *Śrī Śrī Lokanātha.* (Pl. VI, Fig. 11.)
			DALA MARDANA SÀHA.	
75	AR 85 1·12	1676	Small circle in centre; round it a square divided by a svāstika; in circle, trident and two dots; outside the square, above, crescent and sun, to l. flowers, to r. shell and mace. In square, legend *Śrī Śrī Dala Mardana Sāha Deva.* Below, date 888 N.S.	Circle surrounded by eight petals. In circle, sword and wreath on pedestal crescent and sun, and two flowers; in petals, legend *Śrī Śrī Śrī Karunāmaya* (Pl. VI, Fig. 13.)

LIST OF GHORKĀ COINS.

No.	Metal. Weight. Size.	Date. A.D.	Obverse.	Reverse.
			PṚTHVĪ NĀRĀYAṆA SĀHA. (After seizure of territory at Noakoṭ.)	
1	AR 86·5 1·15	1754	(Mohar.) Square, with openings in the middle of the sides, and with small circle in the centre, and divided into four compartments by the four arms of a *svastika*. In central circle, a trident. Around the square; above, sun, moon, and star; to l., *cakra* (discus) and lotus; to r., shell and mace. In square, legend *śrī śrī pṛthvī nārāyaṇa sāha deva*. Below, date 1676 (Śāka era = 1754 A.D.).	Similar to the reverse of the Malla coins of Jaya Bhāskara (No. 22; Pl. III, Fig. 5), Vīra Mahīndra (No. 26; Pl. III, Fig. 9), Jaya Jagajjaya (No. 28; Pl. III, Fig. 11), kings of Kāṭhmāṇḍū; and the obverse of coin of Yoga Prakāśa of Pātan (No. 66; Pl. VI, Fig. 3). Circle surrounded by eight petals. In circle, two straight lines, which represent the imitation Persian characters on the above noted Malla coins, sword and wreath. Legend, in circle, *śrī śrī bhavānī*; in petals, *śrī śrī śrī gorakhanātha*. (Pl. VII, Fig. 1.) *Note.*—From the date this coin was struck by *pṛthvī nārāyaṇa* after his first seizure of Nepal territories at Noakoṭ, and before he conquered the country and took the capitals in 1786 A.D.
2	AR 83 1·10	1769	(As King of Nepal.) (Mohar.) Similar to the preceding. Date, 1695 S.	Similar to the preceding.

No.	Metal. Weight. Size.	Date. A.D.	Obverse.	Reverse.
3	Æ 85 (–)	1773	(Mohar.) Similar to the preceding. Date, 1695 Ś.	Similar to the preceding. But legend in circle, *ŚRI ŚRI LOKANĀTHA*; in petals, *ŚRI ŚRI GORAKHANĀTHA*. (Marsden, MCXXXV.)
4	Æ 41·5 ·77	1771	(Half mohar, or suka.) Imitation Persian characters in two lines. In centre, trident; legend, *ŚRI 3 PṚTHVĪ NĀRĀYAṆA*.	Imitation Persian characters in two lines. In centre, sword and wreath, sun and moon. Legend, *SĀHA DEVA*. Date, 1693 Ś. (Pl. VII, Fig. 2.) *Note.*—The design and symbols of this coin are similar to the mohar of *JAYA NṚPENDRA MALLA* (No. 16; Pl. III, Fig. 1); and with the exception of the symbol on the reverse, to the quarter mohar of *JAYA BHĀSKARA MALLA* (No. 23; Pl. III, Fig. 6).
5	Æ 171 (-)	1771	(Double mohar.) Similar to the mohar No. 1. Date, 1693 Ś.	Similar to the mohar No. 1 (Marsden, MCXXXI). *Note.*—This is the first example of a double mohar.
			Gold Coinage.	
6	AV 85 (–)	1768	(Gold mohar or patlā.) Similar to the silver mohar No. 1. Date, 1690 Ś.	Similar to the silver mohar No. 1 (Marsden, MCXXVII).
7	AV 41·5 (–)	—	(Gold half mohar or sunko-sukā.) Similar to the silver half mohar No. 3.	Similar to the silver half mohar No. 3 (Marsden, MCXXVIII).

No.	Metal. Weight. Size.	Date. A.D.	Obverse.	Reverse.
8	AV 10 (–)	No date.	(Gold eighth of mohar or son-ko-ānī.) Similar to the preceding. No date.	Similar to preceding (Marsden, MCXXVIX).
9	AV 3 (–)		(Gold dām = 1/128 mohar.)	(Marsden, MCXXX.)
10	AV 356 1·25	1771	(Duitole asarfī.) Large gold piece. Similar to mohar No. 1. Date, 1693 Ś.	Circle surrounded by eight-pointed star. Around, ornamental design between each point of the star. In circle, sword and dagger. Legend, in circle, *ŚRĪ* 3, *BHAVĀNĪ*; in points of star, *ŚRĪ ŚRĪ ŚRĪ GORAKHANĀTHA*. (Pl. VII, Fig. 4.)
			(QUEEN NARINDRA LAKṢMĪ DEVĪ.)	
11	AV 22·2 ·63	1771	(Gold sukā.) Offering vase with cover in form of *stūpa*, surmounted by umbrella. Legend, *ŚRĪ ŚRĪ NARĪNDRA LAKṢMĪ DEVĪ.*	Imitation Persian characters in two lines. In centre, trident; above, sun and moon. Legend, *ŚRĪ ŚRĪ BHAVĀNĪ.* Date, 1693 S. Marsden, MCXXXIII. (Pl. VII, Fig. 3.)
			PRATĀPA SIṀHA SĀHA (1774–1777 A.D.).	
12	83 1·15	1774	Device as on mohar of Pṛthvī Nārāyana Sāha, No. 1. Legend, *ŚRĪ ŚRĪ ŚRĪ PRATĀPA SIṀHA SĀHA DEVA.* Date, 1696 Ś.	Device as on No. 1. Legend, in circle, *ŚRĪ ŚRĪ GUHYEŚVARĪ*; in petals, *ŚRĪ ŚRĪ ŚRĪ GORAKHANĀTHA*, as on No 1.
13	AR 42 ·80	1775	(Sukā.) Device as on No. 4, but with crouching lion to l., below. Legend, *ŚRĪ* 2, *PRATĀPA* (lion =) Siṁha.	Device as on No. 4, but with umbrella above. Legend, *SĀHA DEVA.* Date, 1697 Ś. This coin is similar to No. 17. (See Pl. VII, Fig. 5.)

No.	Metal. Weight. Size.	Date. A.D.	Obverse.	Reverse.
14	Æ 10·5 ·53	No date.	(Suki.) None. (Anī.) Sword, without wreath. Legend, *ŚRĪ PRATĀPA.*	Lion to l., with paw raised and tail curled over the back, and flower buds in front. Legend, *SĀHA.* Marsden, MCXXXVIII*c*. (Pl. VII, Fig. 6.)
15	Æ 5·5 ·35	No date.	(Adhānī.) Sword, and legend, *ŚRĪ PRATĀPA.*	Nothing stamped on reverse. Design similar to Malla coin No. 43, of *JAYA PRAKĀŚA MALLA.* (Pl. IV, Fig. 14.)
			Gold Coinage	
16	AV		(Gold mohar or patlā.) Exactly similar to silver mohar No. 12.	Exactly similar to No. 12.
17	AV 41·5 ·77	1775	(Gold sukā.) Exactly similar to silver sukā No. 13.	Exactly similar to silver sukā No. 13. Date, 1697 Ś. Marsden, MCXXXVI. (Pl. VII, Fig. 5.)
18	AV 11·0	No date.	(Gold suki.) None. (Gold ānī.) Exactly similar to silver ānī No. 14.	Exactly similar to silver ānī No. 14. Marsden, MCXXXVIII.
19	AV 5·5 (–)	No date.	(Gold ādhānī.) Same as silver sixteenth of mohar.	Same as silver sixteenth.
20	AV 356 1·25	1776	(Duitole asarfi.) Device as on No. 10. Legend, *ŚRĪ ŚRĪ PRATĀPA SIṀHA SĀHA DEVA.* Date, 1698 Ś.	Similar to the duitole asarfi of Pṛthvī Nārāyaṇa, No. 10.

No.	Metal. Weight. Size.	Date. A.D.	Obverse.	Reverse.
			RĀJENDRA LAKSMĪ DEVĪ (as Queen Consort).	
21	AR 21·5 ·68	1776	(Sukī.) Vase for offerings with cover in form of *stūpa*. Sun and moon. Legend, *ŚRĪ ŚRĪ RĀJENDRA LAKSMĪ DEVĪ.*	Device as on No. 10 of Narindra Lakṣmī Devī. Date, 1698 Ś.
			Gold Coinage.	
22	AV 21·0 ·68	1775	(Gold sukī.) Similar to the preceding.	Similar to the preceding. Date, 1697 Ś. Marsden, MCXL
			RAṆA BAHĀDUR SĀHA (1776–1799 A.D.).	
23	AR 84 1·12	1783	(Mohar.) Device as on No. 1. Legend, *ŚRĪ ŚRĪ ŚRĪ RAṆA BAHĀDUR SĀHA DEVA.* Date, 1705 Ś.	Similar to No. 1.
24	AR 169 ·97	—	(Double mohar.) Similar to the preceding. (Date not noted.)	Similar to the preceding (a small thick coin).
25	AR 41 ·86	1790	(Sukā.) Device as on No. 4. Legend, *ŚRĪ ŚRĪ RAṆA BAHĀDUR.*	Device as on No. 4. Legend, *SĀHA DEVA.* Date, 1712 Ś.
26	AR 19 ·76	1783	(Sukī.) Sword and wreath, two suns, crescents, and stars. Legend, *ŚRĪ RAṆA BAHĀDUR SĀHA DEVA*	Device as on No. 11 Legend, *ŚRĪ ŚRĪ BHAVĀNĪ.* Date, 1705 Ś.
27	AR 11 (–)	No date.	(Ānī.)	Marsden, MCXLII–MCXLIV
28	AR 5·5 (–)	No date.	(Adhānī.)	Marsden, MCXLII–MCXLIV
29	AR ·6	No date.	(Dām.) Minute coins of thin silver.	Marsden, MCXLII–MCXLIV

No.	Metal. Weight. Size.	Date. A.D.	Obverse.	Reverse.
			Gold Coinage.	
30	AV 358 1·25	1796	(Duitole asarfi.) Square surrounded by four petals at the corners and four outer petals at the sides. In outer petals: top, sword and wreath, crescent and sun; to l., *cakra* and lotus; to r., shell and mace. In corner petals, floral device. In square, legend, ŚRĪ ŚRĪ ŚRĪ RAṆA BAHĀDUR SĀHA DEVA. Below, date 1718 Ś.	Similar to No. 10. (Pl. VII, Fig. 7.)
31	AV 85·5 (–)	1778	(Gold mohar or patla.) Exactly similar to silver mohar No. 23. Date, 1700 Ś.	Exactly similar to silver mohar No. 23. Marsden, MCXLII–MCXLIV.
32	AV 41 (–)	1778	(Gold sukā.) Exactly similar to silver half mohar No. 25. Date, 1700 Ś. (Gold sukī.) None. (Gold ānā) None.	Exactly similar to silver half mohar No. 25.
33	AV	—	(Gold dām.) Minute pieces of thin gold leaf, weighing less than a grain.	Marsden, MCXLII–MCXLIV

RĀJENDRA LAKṢMĪ DEVĪ.

(As Queen Regent for her minor son Raṇa Bahādur Sāha.)

No.	Metal. Weight. Size.	Date. A.D.	Obverse.	Reverse.
34	AR 22 ·67	1778	(Quarter mohar.) *Cakra* on pedestal. Legend, ŚRĪ ŚRĪ RĀJENDRA LAKṢMĪ DEVĪ.	Imitation Persian characters in two lines, trident, and two crescents and stars. Legend, ŚRĪ ŚRĪ BHAVĀNĪ. Date, 1700 Ś. Pl. VII, Fig. 8. Marsden, MCXLI (*a*).

No.	Metal. Weight. Size.	Date. A.D.	Obverse.	Reverse.
			RĀJA RĀJEŚVARĪ DEVĪ. (? Slave-girl married by Raṇa Bahādur.)	
35	Æ 21 ·80	1789	(Sukī.) Device as on No. 11, without the umbrella above. Legend, *ŚRĪ* 2, *RĀJA RĀJEŚVARĪ DEVĪ.*	Similar to No. 11. Date, 1711 Ś. *Note.*—There is a similar coin of date 1712. Marsden MCXLV is a similar coin of date 1716 Ś. = 1794 A.D.
			GĪRVANA YUDDHA VIKRAMA SĀHA (1799–1816 A.D.).	
36	Æ 83·5 1·06	1806	(Mohar.) Device as on No. 1 except legend in place of crescent and sun. Legend: above square, *ŚRĪ ŚRĪ ŚRĪ*; within square, *GĪRVĀṆA YUDDHA VIKRAMA SĀHA-DEVA.* Date, 1728 Ś.	Similar to No. 1. But legend in circle, *ŚRĪ* 3, *BHAVĀNĪ.*
37	Æ		(Double mohar.)	
38	Æ 255 1·25		(Large silver coin similar to the duitole asarfi.) Device similar to No. 10, but no *svastika* within the square. Date, 1725 Ś.	Similar to No. 10.
39	Æ		(Half mohar.)	
40	Æ		(Quarter mohar.)	
41	Æ		(Eighth of mohar.)	
42	Æ		(Sixteenth of mohar.)	
43	Æ Square. 34·4 ·6	No date.	"*Svastika* with central circle enclosing trident. Legend, *GĪRVĀṆA YUDDHA VIKRAMA SĀHA DEVA.* No date." *Note.*—The obverse of this coin is the same as the device forming the square on the mohar, and of the same size.	"Circle enclosing dagger (=sword) with wreath, and legend *ŚRĪ BHAVANĪ*; outside circle *ŚRĪ* in each corner (pl. xxviii, 11)."—Catalogue of Coins in the Indian Museum, Calcutta (1906), vol. i, p. 291.

No.	Metal. Weight. Size.	Date. A.D.	Obverse.	Reverse.
			Gold Coinage.	
44	AV 85·5 (–)	1799	(Gold mohar.) Similar to the silver mohar No. 36. Date, 1721 Ś.	Similar to the silver mohar No. 36. Marsden, MCXLVII.
45	AV 356 1·25	—	(Duitole asarfī.) Device as on No. 10.	Similar to No. 10.
46	AV 170 ·94	1799	(Gold double mohar or bakla.) Similar to the silver mohar No. 36. Date, 1721 Ś.	Similar to the silver mohar No. 36. Marsden, MCXLVI.
47	AV 42 ·75	—	(Gold sukā.) Circle surrounded by eight petals. In circle, sword and wreath. In petals, legend *ŚRI ŚRI ŚRI GĪRVĀṆA YUDDHA.*	Small square, inscribed diagonally within large one. In centre square, trident; above outer square, crescent and sun. Legend, above square, *VI*; within square, *KRAMA ŚĀHA*. Date, 1732 Ś. (Pl. VII, Fig. 10.)
48	AV		(Gold sukī.)	
49	AV		(Gold ānī.)	
			(QUEEN) SIDDHI LAKṢMĪ DEVĪ	1810–1814 A.D.).
50	AV 158 ·70		(Baklā, or gold double mohar.)	
51	AV		(Gold sukī.)	
			RĀJENDRA VIKRAMA SĀHA (1816–1847 A.D.).	
52	AR 82·8 1·07	1816	(Mohar.) Device as on No. 1. But with legend *Śrī* above the square. Legend within square, *Śrī Śrī Rājendra Vikram Sāha Deva.* Date, 1738 Ś.	Similar to No. 1.

No.	Metal. Weight. Size.	Date. A.D.	Obverse.	Reverse.
53	AR		(Double mohar.)	
54	AR 42 ·82	1824	(Sukā.) Device as on No. 17. Legend, *Śrī Śrī Śrī Rājendra Vi.*	Device as on No. 17. Legend, *krama Sāha Deva*. Date, 1746.
55	AR		(Quarter mohar.)	
56	AR 6 ·52	No date.	(Ānī.) Sword, crescent, and sun. Legend, *Śrī Rājendra Vi.*	Mace. Legend, *krama Sāha Deva* No date.
57	AR		(Ādhānī.)	
			Gold Coinage.	
58	AV		(Gold mohar.)	
59	AV		(Duitole asarfi.) Of same denomination as No. 10.	
60	AV		(Baklā, or gold double mohar.)	
61	AV		(Gold sukā.)	
62	AV		(Gold sukī.)	
63	AV		(Gold ānī.)	

(QUEENS) LAKṢMĪ DEVĪ AND SUNDARĪ DEVĪ (1816–1832 A.D.)

No.	Metal. Weight. Size.	Date. A.D.	Obverse.	Reverse.
64	AR		(Sukī.)	
65	AR		(Ānī.)	
			Gold Coinage.	
66	AV		(Baklā, or gold double mohar.)	
67	AV		(Gold sukī.)	
68	AV		(Gold ānī.)	

No.	Metal. Weight. Size.	Date. A.D.	Obverse.	Reverse.
			QUEEN (SAMRÂJYA) LAKṢMÎ DEVÎ.	
69	Æ 20·6 ·76	1824	(Sukī.) Vase for offerings with cover in form of *stūpa*, with flowers on either side. Legend, *Śrī Samrājya Lakṣmī Devī*.	Imitation Persian characters in two lines. In centre, trident; above, crescent and sun. Legend, *Śrī Śrī Bhavānī*. Date, 1746 Ś. *Note.*—This coin is wrongly described in the Catalogue of the Indian Museum, Calcutta, as "Humped bull r." (C.C.I.M.C., vol. i, p. 291, and pl. xxviii, fig. 12). From the plate it appears that a lump of metal has stuck on to the coin, partly concealing the trident, and this has been taken for a "humped bull."
			SURENDRA VIKRAMA SÂHA (1847–1881 A.D.).	
70	Æ 85·2 1·1	1849	(Mohar.) Device as on No. 1, but with legend *Śrī* above the square, in place of crescent and sun. Legend within the square, *Śrī Śrī Surendra Vikrama Śāha Deva*. Date, 1771 Ś.	Similar to No. 1.
71	Æ		(Double mohar.)	
72	Æ ·42 ·8	No date.	(Sukā.) Imitation Persian character in two lines. In centre, trident. Legend, *Śrī Śrī Śrī Surendra Vi*.	Imitation Persian characters in two lines. Legend, *krama Sāha Deva*.
73	Æ	No date.	(Sukī.)	

No.	Metal. Weight. Size.	Date. A.D.	Obverse.	Reverse.
74	Æ 10·7 ·6	No date.	(Ānī.) In centre, sword; above, crescent and sun. Legend, *Śrī Surendra Vi.*	In centre, mace; above, two pellets. Legend, *krama Sāha Deva.*
75	Æ 5·2 ·5	No date.	(Ādhānī.) Similar to preceding.	Similar to preceding.
76	Æ 2·1 ·4	No date.	(Paisā.) Similar to preceding.	Nothing on the reverse: these coins are so thin that the die of the obverse shows through.
77	Æ ·35 ·30 to ·35	No date.	(Phokā dām or cūn dām = $\frac{1}{128}$ of a mohar.) Minute coins on silver leaf. Similar to preceding.	Similar to the preceding.
			Gold Coinage.	
78	AV 85·3 1·04	1816	(Gold mohar.) Similar to the silver mohar No. 70. Date, 1738 S.	Similar to the silver mohar No. 70.
79	AV 356 1·23	1847	(Large gold coin.) Circle surrounded by triple lines, forming an eight-pointed star. In circle, sword and wreath; in the points of the star, pellets; in the outer angles, above, crescent and sun; to l., *cakra* and lotus; to r., shell and mace. Legend, in circle, *Śrī Śrī Surendra Vikrama Sāha Deva.* Date below, 1769 S.	Similar to No. 10. (Pl. VII, Fig. 9.)
80	AV	—	(Baklā, gold double mohar.)	

No.	Metal. Weight. Size.	Date. A.D.	Obverse.	Reverse.
81	AV 42 ·8	No date.	(Gold sukā.) Similar to silver sukā No. 72.	Similar to silver sukā No. 72.
82		No date.	(Gold sukī.)	
83			(Gold ānī.) Similar to silver ānī No. 74.	Similar to silver ānī No. 74.
84			(Gold ādhānī.) Similar to silver No. 75.	Similar to silver No. 75.
85			(Gold pai, one thirty-secondth of a mohar.)	
86			(Phokā dām or cūṇ dām.) Minute gold coins similar to No. 77.	
			(QUEEN) TRAILOKYARĀJA LAKSMĪ DEVĪ.	
87	AR 20·5 ·75	1847	(Sukī.) Device as on No. 11. Legend, *Srī Trailokya Lakṣmī Devī.*	Device as on No. 11, but with two crescents and dots. Legend, *Śrī Śrī Bhavānī.* Date, 1769 Ś.
			Gold Coinage.	
88	AV	1849	(Gold mohar.) Date, 1771 S.	
89	AV	—	(Gold sukī.) Similar to silver No. 87.	Similar to silver No. 87.
			(QUEEN) SURA RĀJA LAKṢMĪ DEVĪ.	
90	AV 21·2 ·74		(Gold sukī.) Indian Museum, Calcutta. "Temple" (should be, vase for offerings with cover in form of *stūpa*) "between flowers in centre; in field, legend *Śrī Sura Rāja Lakṣmī Devī.*"	"Central circle enclosing trident. Legend, in field, *Śrī Śrī Bhavānī,* 1790. In mint condition. (Pl. xxviii, 13.)" C.C.I.M.C., p. 292.

No.	Metal. Weight. Size.	Date. A.D.	Obverse.	Reverse.
			Copper Coinage.	
91	Æ 153 1·1	1876	(Dāk = sixteenth of mohar.) In centre, plain square. Ornamental design in upper and lateral marginal spaces. Legend in square, *Śrī Śrī Surendra Vikrama Sāha Deva.* Date below, 1798 Ś.	In centre, plain square, ornamental design in surrounding spaces. Legend in square, *Śrī Śrī Śrī Nepāl Sarkār,* "Government of Nepal." (Device similar to No. 88, *vide* Pl. VII, Fig. 11.)
92	Æ 73 ·9	1873	(Paisā = thirty-secondth of mohar.) Similar to the preceding. Date, 1795 Ś.	Similar to the preceding. (Pl. VII, Fig. 11.)
93	Æ 17·5 to 20 ·52	1871	(Copper dām.) No device. Legend, *Śrī Nepāl.*	No device. Legend, *Sarkār.* Date, 93 Ś.

PṚTHVĪ VĪRA VIKRAMA SĀHA (1881 A.D.). The present king.

No.	Metal. Weight. Size.	Date. A.D.	Obverse.	Reverse.
94	Ꝛ 82·5 1·02	1883	(Mohar.) Device as on No. 1, but with legend *Śrī Śrī* above in place of crescent and sun. Legend, in square, *Śrī Pṛthvī Vīra Vikrama Sāha Deva.* Date below, 1805 Ś. *Note.*—This is a smaller coin than his subsequent mohars. The side of the square is only ·52 inch, and the legend is in smaller letters.	Similar to No. 1.
95	Ꝛ 85·2 1	1899	Similar to the preceding, but larger square, and legend in larger letters. Date, 1821 Ś.	Similar to the preceding.
96	Ꝛ 340 1·11	1895	(Four mohar.) Similar to the mohar No. 94. Date, 1817 Ś.	Similar to the mohar No. 94. *Note.*—This coin is ·12 inch in thickness.

No.	Metal. Weight. Size.	Date. A.D.	Obverse.	Reverse.
97	Æ 170·5 1·08		(Double mohar.) Similar to mohar No. 94. Date, 1811 Ś.	
98	Æ 42·4 ·85	1895	(Sukā.) Trident in small central circle. On either side: above, crescent and sun; below, two flowers. Legend, *Śrī Śrī Pṛthvī Vīra Vikrama Sāha Deva.*	Imitation Persian characters in two lines. In centre, sword and wreath. Ornamented with two groups of three pellets above and also below, and two of four pellets in centre. Legend, *krama Sāha Deva.* 1817 Ś.
99	Æ 21·2 ·73		(Sukī.) Vase for offerings with cover in form of *stūpa.* Legend, *Śrī Pṛthvī Vīra Vikrama Sāha Deva.*	Trident in small central circle. Above, on either side, crescent and sun. Legend in field, *Śrī Śrī Bharānī.*
100	Æ 11·5 ·50	No date.	(Ānī.) In centre, sword; above, to l. crescent, to r. dot for sun. Legend, *Śrī Pṛthvī Vīra Vi.*	In centre, mace. Legend, *krama Sāha Deva.*
101	Æ 5·2 ·45		(Ādhānī.) Similar to the preceding.	Similar to the preceing.
102	Æ 2·1 ·4		(Paisā mohar.) In centre, sword. Legend, *Śrī Pṛthvī Vīra.*	No device. The coin is so thin that the die of the obverse shows through.
103	Æ ·35 ·35		(Phokā dām. or cun dām.) Minute silver coin, similar to the preceding.	Similar to the preceding. *Note.*—This coin is of same denomination as No 77 of Surendra Vikrama Sāha.

No.	Metal. Weight. Size.	Date. A.D.	Obverse.	Reverse.
			Gold Coinage.	
104	AV		(Gold mohar.) Similar to silver mohar No. 95.	
105	AV		(Duitole asarfī.) Large gold coin of same type as No. 10.	
106	AV		(Gold sukā.)	
107	AV		(Gold sukī.)	
108	AV		(Gold ānī.)	
109	AV		(Gold ādhānī.)	
110	AV		(Gold pai.)	
111	AV		(Minute pieces of gold leaf.)	
			Copper Coinage.	
112	Æ		(Dāk = sixteenth of mohar.) Similar to paisā No. 113.	Similar to paisā No. 113.
113	Æ 76·5 ·87	1894	(Paisā = thirty-secondth of mohar.) Device similar to dāk and paisā of Surendra Vikrama Sāha (Pl. VII, Fig. 11), but with crescent and sun and legend *Śrī* in place of ornament. Legend, as noted above, *Śrī*; in square, 5, *Pṛthvī Vīra Vikrama Sāha Deva*. Date below, 1951 (Saṁvat).	Plain square. In margin: above, crescent and sun; on sides and below, ornamental design. Legend: above, *Śrī*; in square, ***Paśupati Nātha Nepal*** ("Paśupati, Lord of Nepal").
114	Æ		(Dāk = sixteenth of mohar.) Device and legend similar to paisā No. 115.	Similar to paisā No. 115 (*vide* Pl. VII, Fig. 13)

No.	Metal. Weight. Size.	Date. A.D.	Obverse.	Reverse.
115	Æ 82·3 ·9	1893	(Paisā = thirty-secondth of mohar.) Circle, surrounded by eight-pointed star, within a scolloped border, containing crescent · between each point of the star. Within circle two *kukhris* (Gorkhā knives) crossed, above them *pādukā* (footprints of Viṣṇu), and around, legend *Srī* 5, *Pṛthvī Vīra Vikrama Sāha Deva.*	Within circle, surrounded by eight-pointed star and ornamental border, as on the obverse, small central circle, containing trident. Legend around central circle, *Śrī* 5, *Bhavānī* (date, 1950 Saṁvat), *Gorkhā Sarkār.* (Pl. VII, Fig. 13.)
116			(Paisā = thirty-secondth of mohar.) Within a rudely-formed wreath, legend *Srī* 5, *Pṛthvī Vīra Vikrama Sāha Deva.*	Within rude wreath, legend *Śrī* 5 *Bhavānī Nepāl Sarkār.* Date, 1953 Saṁvat. (Pl. VII, Fig. 12.) *Note.* — The obverse and reverse of this coin are transposed on the Plate.

TABLE I.—CONTEMPORARY LIST OF THE KINGS OF BHĀTGĀON, KĀTHMĀṆḌU, AND PĀTAN, FROM THE DIVISION OF THE KINGDOM ON THE DEATH OF YAKSHA MALLA (*circa* 1460 A.D.) TO THE GORKHA CONQUEST.

KINGDOM OF BHĀTGĀON.			KINGDOM OF KĀTHMĀṆḌU.			KINGDOM OF BANEPA.		
No.	Date. A.D.	Name of King.	No.	Date. A.D.	Name of King.	No.	Date. A.D.	Name of King.
1	1496	Rāya-malla.	1		Ratna.	1	—	Jayarana-malla.
2	—	Bhuvana-malla.	2		Amara.			
3	1524-33	Jita-malla and Prāṇa-malla (joint regency).	3		Sūrya.			
4	—	Prāṇa-malla (sole king).	4	1531	Narendra.			
5	—	Viśva-malla.	5	1566	Jaya-Mahendra.			
6	1572 80	Trailokya-malla.	6	1575-6	Sadāśiva.	KINGDOM OF PĀTAN *or* LALITAPUR.		
7	1617 33	Jagajjyotir-malla.	7	1600	Śivadeva or Śivasiṁha.			
8	—	Narendra.	8		Hariharasiṁha.	1		Hariharasiṁha.
9	1642	Jagatprakāśa Malla.	9		Lakṣmīnara Siṁha.	2	1631	Siddhi Narasiṁha.
			10	1649	Pratāpa Malla (Queen Rupamatī Devī).	3	1655	Śrīnivāsa.

10	1663	Jitamitra Malla.	11	1669	{Cakravartindra or Jaya {Cakra Mahendra.			
			12	1674	Nṛpendra or Jaya Nṛpendra.			
			13		Mahipendra.			
			14	1682	Pārthivendra.			
			15	1682	Jaya Bhupālendra.	4	1686	Yoga Narendra or Yogendra.
11	1696	Bhūpatindra.	16	1697	Jaya Bhāskara.	5	1705	Jaya Loka Prakāśa (Queen dowager Yogamati).
						6	1706	Jaya Indra.
			17	1708	Jaya Vīra Mahīndra or Mahindra Siṁha Deva.	7	—	Jaya Vīra Mahindra or Mahindra Siṁha Deva
						8	1720	Hṛdi Narasiṁha.
12	1722	Jaya Raṇajita.	18	1722	Jaya Jagajjaya styled Mahipatindra).	9	1722	Jaya Yoga Prakāśa.
			19	1726		10	1729	Jaya Viṣṇu.
					Pāṭan).	11	1742	Rajya Prakāśa.
			20	1749	[Jyoti Prakāśa.] Coin struck apparently in a rebellion; see Wright, p. 224.	12	1752	Viśvajita.
						13	1768	Dala Mardana Sāha.

PLATE 1.

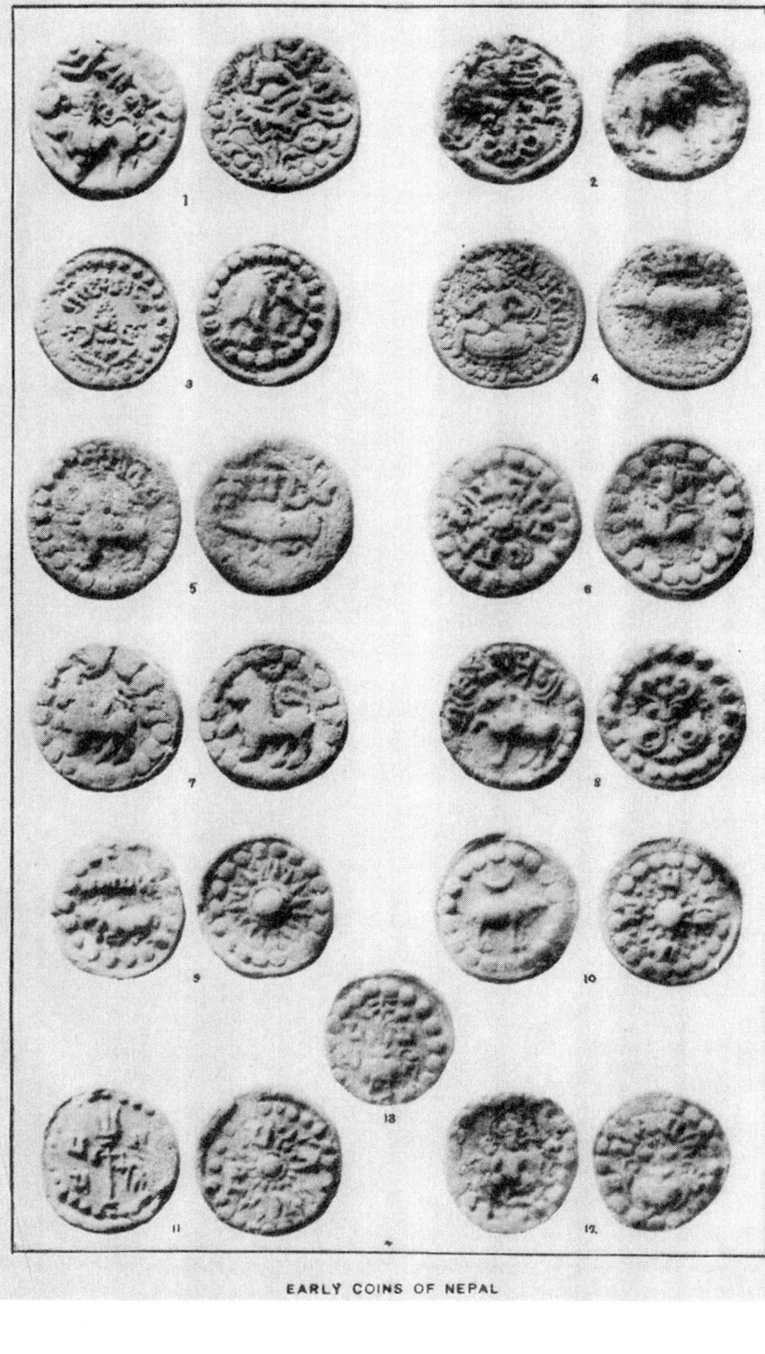

EARLY COINS OF NEPAL

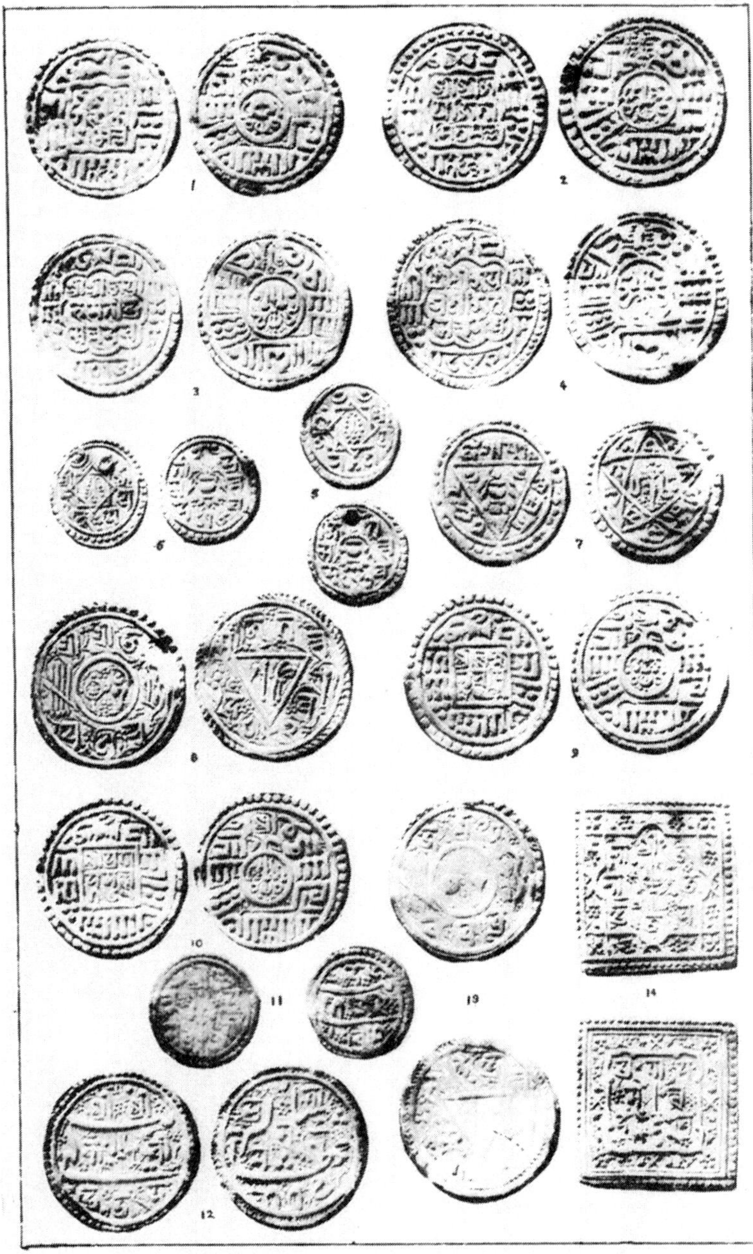

MALLA COINS OF BHĀTGAON AND KĀTHMĀNDŪ.

PLATE III.

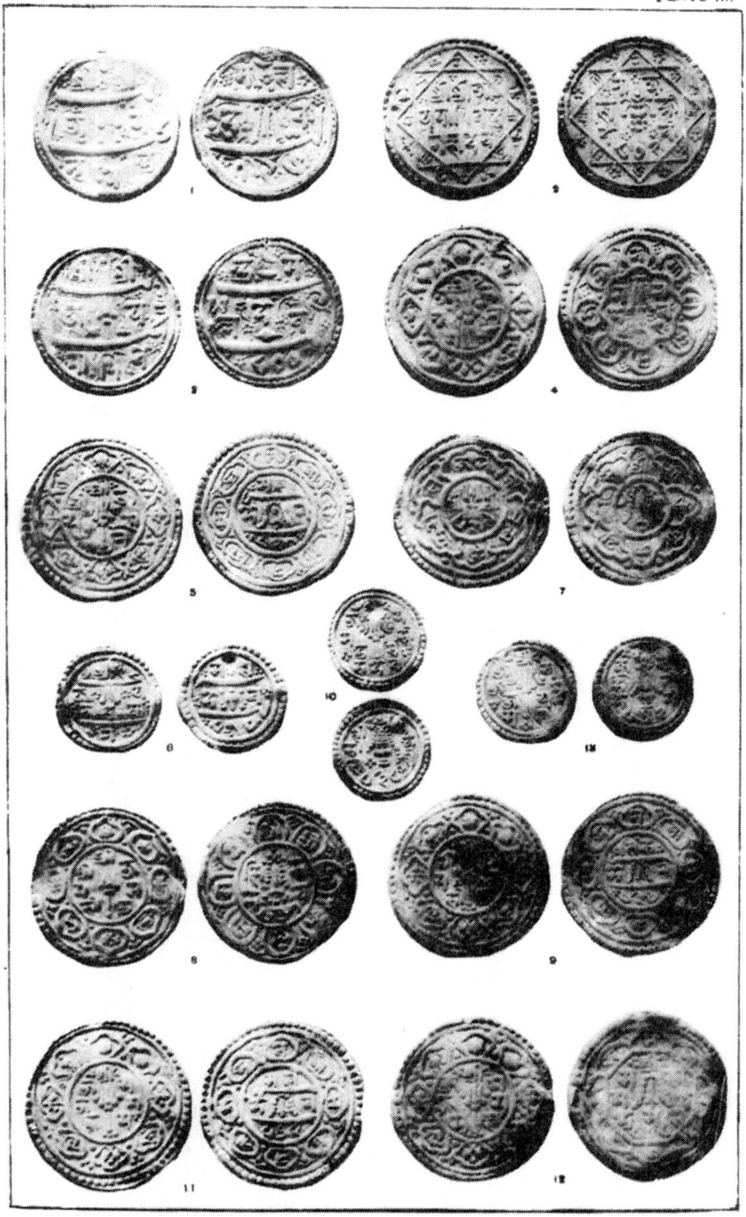

MALLA COINS OF KĀTHMĀNDŪ (CONTINUED.)

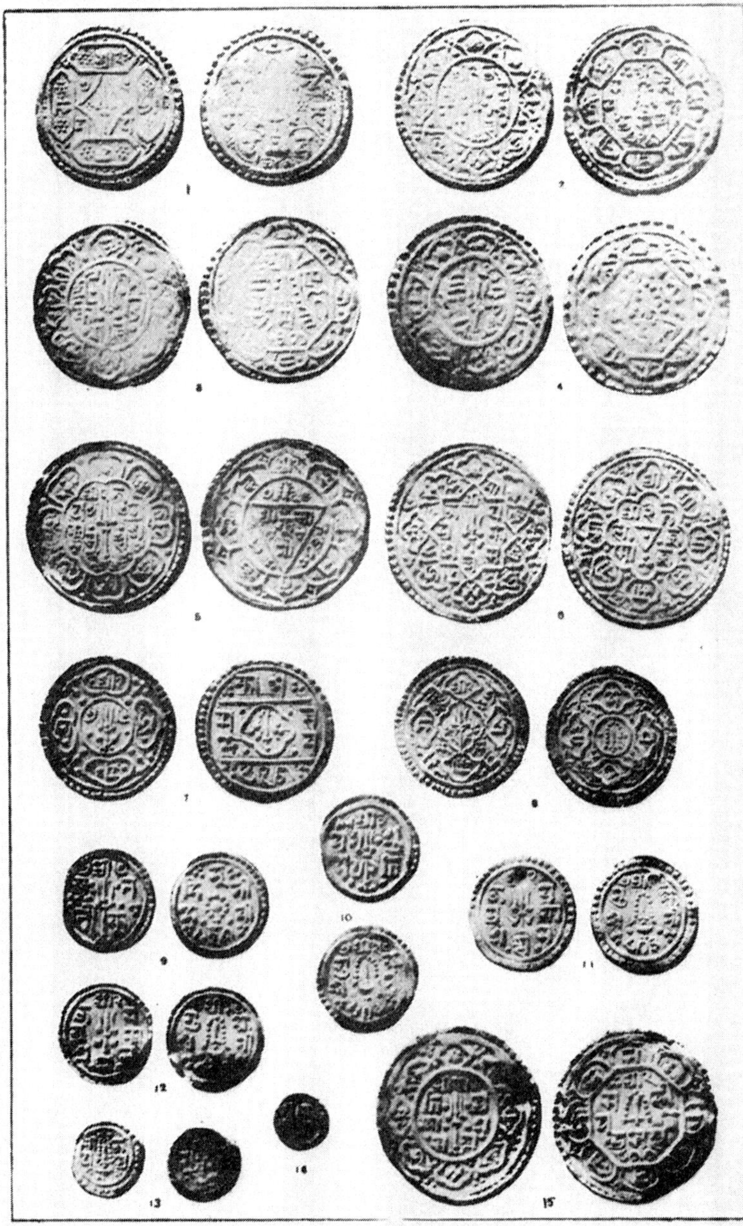

MALLA COINS OF KATHMÂNDÛ (CONTINUED)

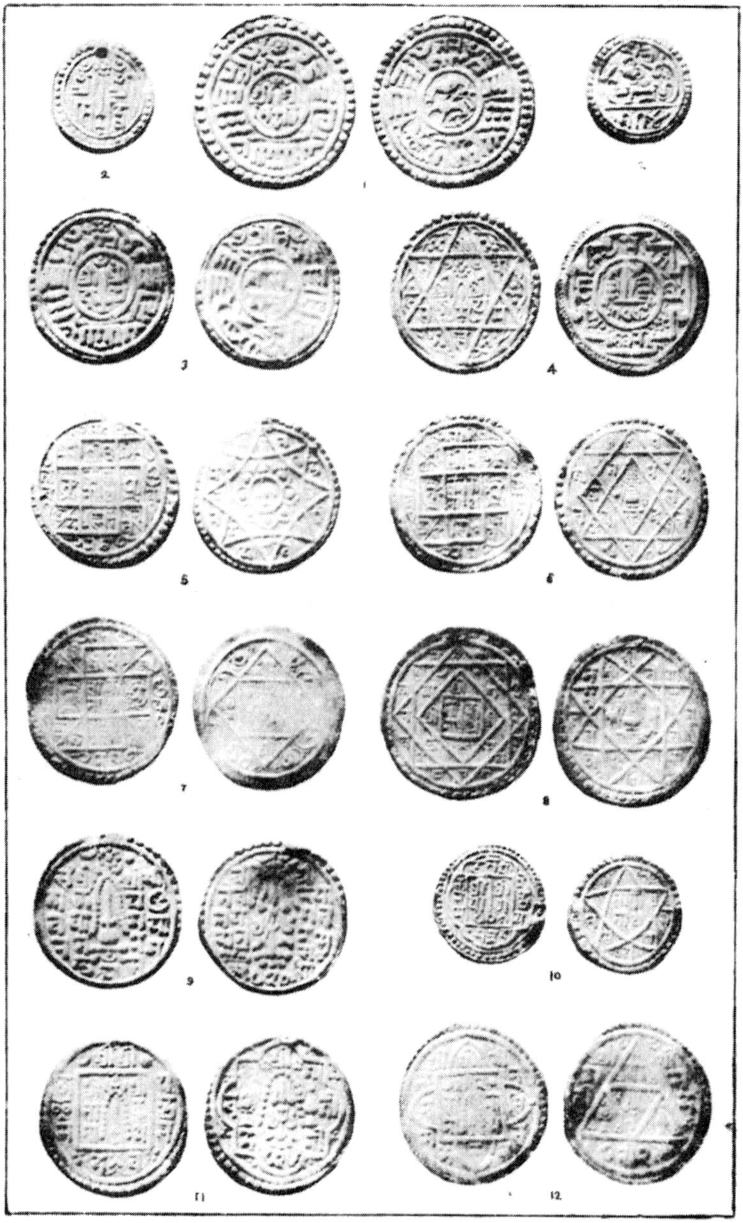

MALLA COINS OF PATAN

MALLA COINS OF PĀTAN (CONTINUED.)

PLATE VII.

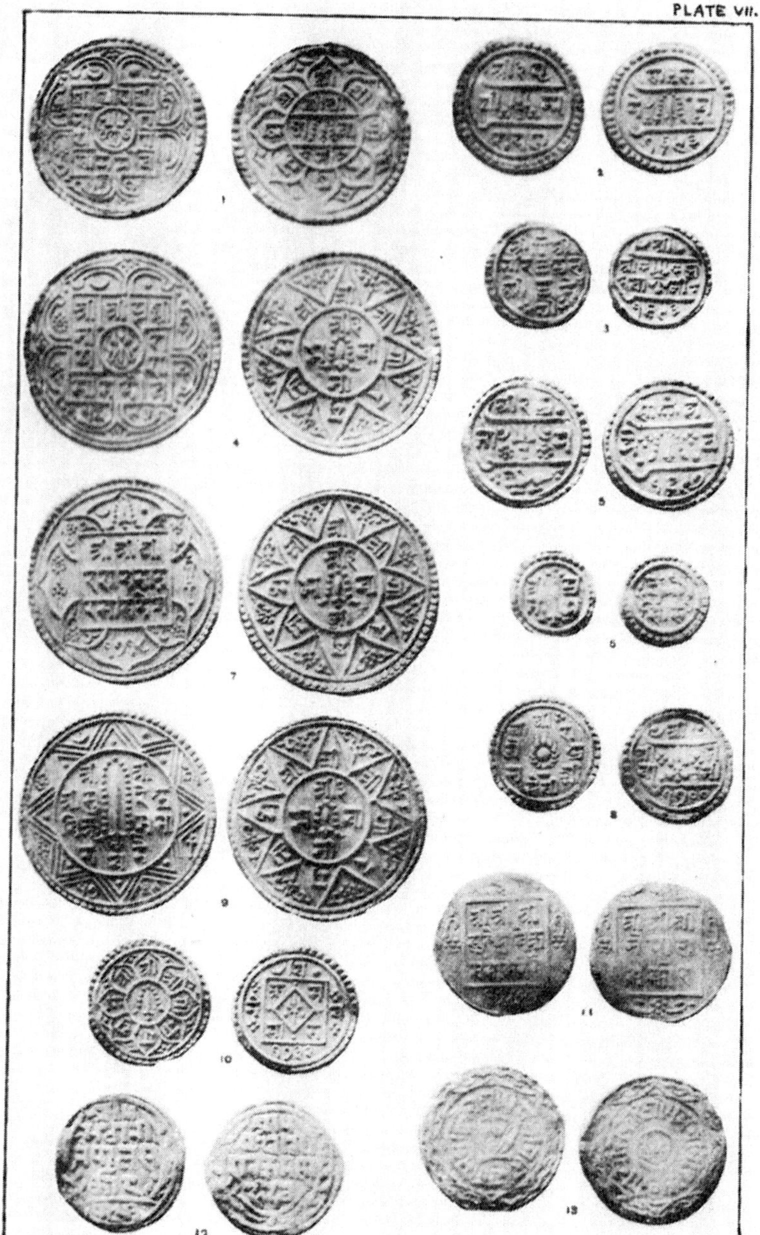

GORKHA COINS.

Published by

Facsimile Publisher
Ashok Vihar, Delhi-110052 (India)
Website: www.facsimilepublisher.com

Distributed by

Gyan Books Pvt. Ltd.
5, Ansari Road, Daryaganj, New Delhi-110002 (India)
E-mail: books@gyanbooks.com, Website: www.gyanbooks.com

2 222000 002701